THE UNITED NATIONS AND
INTERNATIONAL POLITICS

STUDIES IN CONTEMPORARY HISTORY

Series Editors: T. G. Fraser and J. O. Springhall

THE ARAB–ISRAELI CONFLICT
T. G. Fraser

THE ULSTER QUESTION SINCE 1945
James Loughlin

THE RISE AND FALL OF THE SOVIET EMPIRE
Raymond Pearson

THE CIVIL RIGHTS MOVEMENT: Struggle and Resistance
William T. Martin Riches

THE UNITED NATIONS AND INTERNATIONAL POLITICS
Stephen Ryan

JAPAN SINCE 1945
Dennis B. Smith

THE UNITED NATIONS AND INTERNATIONAL POLITICS

STEPHEN RYAN

St. Martin's Press
New York

St. Martin's Press, Scholarly and Reference Division, 175 Fifth Avenue, New York, N.Y. 10010

First published in the United States of America in 2000

This book is printed on paper suitable for recycling and made from fully managed and sustained forest sources.

Printed in Hong Kong

ISBN 0–312–22824–4 clothbound
ISBN 0–312–22825–2 paperback

Library of Congress Cataloging-in-Publication Data
Ryan, Stephen, 1956–
The United Nations and international politics / Stephen Ryan.
p. cm. — (Studies in contemporary history)
Includes bibliographical references and index.
ISBN 0–312–22824–4 (cl.). — ISBN 0–312–22825–2 (pbk.)
1. United Nations.   2. World politics—1945–   I. Title.
II. Series: Studies in contemporary history (New York, N.Y.)
JZ4984.5.R93   1999
341.23'09—dc21
                                                    99–37894
                                                    CIP

CONTENTS

Contents

Contents

Conclusion: New Horizons and Old Restrictions

SERIES EDITORS' PREFACE

There are those, politicians among them, who feel that historians should not teach or write about contemporary events and people – many of whom are still living – because of the difficulty of treating such matters with historical perspective, that it is right to draw some distinction between the study of history and the study of current affairs. Proponents of this view seem to be unaware of the concept of contemporary history to which this series is devoted, that the history of the recent past can and should be written with a degree of objectivity. As memories of the Second World War recede, it is surely time to place in perspective the postwar history that has shaped all our lives, whether we were born in the 1940s or the 1970s.

Many countries – Britain, the United States and Germany among them – allow access to their public records under a thirty-year rule, opening up much of the postwar period to archival research. For more recent events, diaries, memoirs, and the investigations of newspapers and television, confirm the view of the famous historian Sir Lewis Namier that all secrets are in print provided you know where to look for them. Contemporary historians also have the opportunity, denied to historians of earlier periods, of interviewing participants in the events they are analysing. The problem facing the contemporary historian is, if anything, the embarrassment of riches.

In any case, the nature and extent of world changes since the late 1980s have clearly signalled the need for concise discussion of major themes in post-1945 history. For many of us the difficult thing to grasp is how dramatically the world has changed over recent years: the collapse of the Soviet Union and Russian communism; the end of Soviet hegemony over eastern Europe; the unification of Germany; the end of the Cold War; America's sense of a 'new world order'; the pace of integration in the European Community; the disintegration of Yugoslavia; the Middle East peace settlement; the continuing economic strength of Japan. Writing in a structured and cogent way about these seismic changes is what makes contemporary history so challenging, and we hope that the end result will convey some of this excitement and interest to our readers.

The general objective of this series, written entirely by members of the School of History, Philosophy and Politics of the University of Ulster, is to offer concise and up-to-date treatments of postwar themes considered of historical and political significance, and to stimulate critical thought about the theoretical assumptions and conceptual apparatus underlying interpretation of the topics under discussion. The series should bring some of the central themes and problems confronting students and teachers of recent history, politics and international affairs into sharper focus than the textbook writer alone could provide. The blend required to write contemporary history that is both readable and easily understood but also accurate and scholarly is not easy to achieve, but we hope that this series will prove worthwhile for both students and teachers interested in world affairs.

University of Ulster
                                            T. G. FRASER
                                            J. O. SPRINGHALL

ACKNOWLEDGEMENTS

I am pleased to be able to offer my thanks to a number of people. The series editors invited me to contribute this book and made useful suggestions for changes to the first draft. The Faculty of Humanities at the University of Ulster gave me study leave to research and write it. The library staff at Magee College ensured an efficient and courteous delivery of material. Jonathan Reeve at Macmillan was patient in the face of several changes to the delivery date caused by pressures of work, illness and the arrival of a daughter called Lara. Above all, my special thanks to Clionagh.

STEPHEN RYAN

This book is dedicated to
Clionagh, Naoise, Sorcha and Lara

LIST OF ABBREVIATIONS

CAMDUN	Conference on a More Democratic United Nations
ECA	Economic Commission for Africa
ECAP	Economic Commission for Asia and the Pacific
ECE	Economic Commission for Europe
ECLA	Economic Commission for Latin America
ECOMOG	Economic Community Military Observer Group
ECOSOC	Economic and Social Council
ECWA	Economic Commission for West Africa
FAO	Food and Agriculture Organization
G-77	Group of 77
GATT	General Agreement on Tariffs and Trade
HRC	Human Rights Commission
HRFOR	Human Rights Field Operation
IAEA	International Atomic Energy Agency
IBRD (World Bank)	International Bank for Reconstruction and Development
ICJ	International Court of Justice
ICTFY	International Criminal Tribunal for the Former Yugoslavia
I-FOR	International Force
ILC	International Law Commission
ILO	International Labour Organization
IMF	International Monetary Fund
IPTF	International Police Task Force

MICIVIH	International Civilian Mission to Haiti
MINUGUA	United Nations Verification Mission in Guatemala
MINURSO	United Nations Mission for the Referendum in Western Sahara
MIPONUH	United Nations Civilian Police Mission in Haiti
MNF	Multinational Force (in Lebanon)
NATO	North Atlantic Treaty Organization
NGO	Non-Governmental Organization
NIEO	New International Economic Order
OAS	Organization of American States
ONUC	United Nations Operation in Congo
ONUCA	United Nations Observer Group in Central America
ONUMOZ	United Nations Operation in Mozambique
ONUSAL	United Nations Observer Mission in El Salvador
ONUVEN	United Nations Verification of Elections in Nicaragua
PLO	Palestine Liberation Organization
S-FOR	Stabilization Force
SWAPO	South West African Peoples' Organization
UNAMIR	United Nations Assistance Mission for Rwanda
UNAVEM	United Nations Angola Verification Mission
UNCED	United Nations Conference on the Environment and Development
UNCIP	United Nations Commission for India and Pakistan
UNCRO	United Nations Confidence Restoration Operation
UNCTAD	United Nations Conference on Trade and Development

UNDOF	United Nations Disengagement Observer Force
UNDP	United Nations Development Programme
UNDRO	United Nations Disaster Relief Organization
UNEF	United Nations Emergency Force
UNEP	United Nations Environment Programme
UNESCO	United Nations Educational, Scientific and Cultural Organization
UNFICYP	United Nations Force in Cyprus
UNHCR	United Nations High Commissioner for Refugees
UNICEF	United Nations Children's Fund
UNIFIL	United Nations Interim Force in Lebanon
UNIIMOG	United Nations Iran–Iraq Military Observer Group
UNIKOM	United Nations Iraq–Kuwait Observer Mission
UNITAF	United Task Force in Somalia
UNMIBH	United Nations Mission in Bosnia and Herzegovina
UNMIH	United Nations Mission in Haiti
UNMOGIP	United Nations Military Observer Group in India and Pakistan
UNMOP	United Nations Mission of Observers in Prevlaka
UNOGIL	United Nations Observer Group in Lebanon
UNOMIL	United Nations Observer Mission in Liberia
UNOMUR	United Nations Observer Mission in Uganda–Rwanda
UNOMOZ	United Nations Operation in Mozambique

UNOSOM	United Nations Operation in Somalia
UNOVER	United Nations Observer Mission to Verify the Elections in Eritrea
UNPA	United Nations Protected Area
UNPREDEP	United Nations Preventive Deployment Force
UNPROFOR	United Nations Protection Force
UNRWA	United Nations Relief and Works Agency
UNSCOB	United Nations Special Committee on the Balkans
UNSCOM	United Nations Special Commission
UNSCOP	United Nations Special Committee on Palestine
UNSF	United Nations Security Force
UNSMIH	United Nations Support Mission in Haiti
UNTAC	United Nations Transitional Authority in Cambodia
UNTAES	United Nations Transitional Administration for Eastern Slavonia
UNTAG	United Nations Transition Assistance Group
UNTEA	United Nations Temporary Executive Authority in West Irian
UNTMIH	United Nations Temporary Mission in Haiti
UNTSO	United Nations Truce Supervision Organization
WFP	World Food Programme
WHO	World Health Organization

INTRODUCTION

> In the sacred drama by the East River, the realities and fantasies of international life mingle, collide and take new shapes from interaction. The process ought surely to attract more serious interest than it has so far done. (O'Brien, 1968: 299)

The United Nations (UN), as its own publicity is fond of pointing out, is a small organization by most standards. The whole system employs about the same number of people as Disney World and Disneyland and only one-third of the number of people who work for Macdonald's. The budget for its core functions is 4 per cent of New York City's annual budget and is less than the annual budget of the Tokyo fire department (Hannay, 1996). The UN Secretariat employs a quarter of the number of civil servants working in the state of Wyoming. The total cost of all peacekeeping operations in 1995 was less than 0.3 per cent of world-wide military expenditure and the whole UN system costs about $2 per person living on this planet. Put another way, this is what is spent in Britain on alcohol every 15 weeks (Fisas, 1995: 5).

Yet, of course, the worth of the UN cannot be measured in these crude terms. In 1945 many hoped that this new body would be a major player in the fight against the evils of war and human rights abuse, problems vividly imprinted on the memories of those who had lived through the first half of the twentieth century. Perhaps no other international organization has had invested in it so much hope for a better world or has provoked so much disappointment by its own shortcomings.

Of course, there has been too much easy optimism about the UN. O'Brien (1968) reminds us of this when he distinguishes the real UN from the 'Platonic UN'. The latter he characterizes as an imaginary world government that 'always turns on a core of delusion' as opposed to the existing UN which 'has yet a core of sense, in the instinct for survival in the world as it is'. All mention of fundamental reform of the UN O'Brien (1968: 245) calls the 'paraphernalia of the Platonic United Nations' and diverts us from the more urgent question of what we can do now 'to make the best use of the actual possibilities of that institution' (O'Brien, 1968: 274).

So what is this United Nations? According to Claude (1996: 290–1), there are really two interdependent UNs. The 'First UN' is made up of the staff at UN headquarters in New York and other offices around the globe. This has a corporate identity and its chief is the Secretary-General. The 'Second UN' is a 'collectivity formed by almost all the states of the world' and is where the real power resides. The Secretary-General, although head of the first UN, is the chief employee of this collectivity. The first UN can be described as an 'it', the second UN as 'we'. This distinction is even made by member states themselves, who sometimes treat the UN as an entity external to themselves (Claude, 1984: 10). The language of the first UN is internationalism and global interest, the second UN may sometimes use similar words but its discourse is mainly about *raison d'état*. Although the first UN remains rooted in the second, Roberts and Kingsbury (1994: 24) claim that the organization is 'more than the sum of its parts' and 'has developed a life and an ethos of its own'. For whereas individual states are primarily motivated by the pursuit of their own interests the UN can, sometimes, rise over these concerns to focus on the global or planetary perspective.

However, there is one important qualification that has to be made to Claude's assessment. Whereas it may be true that the UN can be distinguished from its member states and in this sense can be called an 'it', this should not lead us to believe that the organization has a single voice and a common

2

purpose. It is more accurate to refer to the UN as a system, which 'like governments, consists of executive, legislative, administrative, and judicial agencies at its centre and numerous specialized agencies in the field that are relatively autonomous of its central organs' (Rosenau, 1992: 44).

A recent study by Kratochwil and Ruggie (1997) suggest, that the literature on international organizations offers four ways of studying international governance. They are: the study of formal institutions; the analysis of institutional practices ('actual' decision-making); the role of the organization within a 'more broadly conceived process of international governance'; and – as a component of regime analysis – the arrangements established to co-ordinate and organize aspects of international behaviour. We will touch on all four approaches in this study. It is necessary to set out the formal structure of the UN and to see how this was adapted when it came up against Cold War realities. We shall also see how the UN has contributed to the creation and maintenance of regimes in the areas of security, human rights and the environment. However, the emphasis here will be on the third approach, which is concerned with questions such as the role of the UN in resolving international problems and how this body reflects, magnifies or modifies characteristic features of the international system (Kratochwil and Ruggie, 1997). This perspective allows us to consider the UN as both a product of changing international relations and as an agent and catalyst of this change. To do full justice to this way of studying the UN it is necessary to take an historical perspective. This way of looking at the UN has certain advantages identified by Goodrich (1976: 4–5). These are: it helps to establish the historical record on which to base evaluation and so places normative judgements on a surer foundation; it puts the present in perspective; and it should provide some basis for judging the course of future developments.

Roberts and Kingsbury (1994: 9) claim that 'in the half century since its foundation in 1945, the United Nations has been a central institution in the conduct of international relations.' This is probably too flattering. On the other hand there are some critics of the UN who seem to believe not only that it is ineffectual, but that it hinders global improvements. Bertrand (1994: 474), for example, claims that 'the existence of the UN, and the belief that this obsolete institution can and should play a role, is in fact a serious obstacle to the remodelling of ways of thinking.' The truth lies somewhere between these two judgements.

1

CREATION

Now there is the effort of the new men. They apply a new test and pursue a new purpose. They are not influenced by national greed or national pride. They apply the test of international advantage and the test of the interests of the common people concerned. That is a new thing in the world. (Hugh Foot, 1964: 245)

Many writers have noted how the development of organizations such as the League of Nations and the United Nations drew on some important features of interstate relations in the nineteenth century (Claude, 1984; Groom, 1988; Nicholas, 1959; Zimmern, 1939). Three of these have received particular attention. The first was the idea of a Concert of powers that emerged after the Vienna Conference that ended the Napoleonic Wars. The Concert idea can itself be seen as a development of the practice of convening conferences at the end of wars to discuss what we would now call security issues. These include the meetings in Westphalia in 1648, after the Thirty Years War, and in Utrecht in 1713 at the end of the War of the Spanish Succession.

With the Concert system we find a recognition that great powers had a special responsibility for regulating international politics. Although different states had competing views on the role of this Concert, in the years after Napoleon's defeat it did seem to provide a degree of order (Hall, 1996: 82). A number of meetings were held between 1815 and 1822 to discuss issues such as the reintegration of France into the European system (Aix-la-Chapelle, 1818) and uprisings in Italy (Troppau, 1820). Even though this system broke up in the 1820s because of tensions between the more liberal British and the more conservative Austrians, meetings involving the great powers continued to be convened to discuss matters of international concern. Such meetings included the London Conference in 1830 that decided the future of Belgium and the Berlin Conference of 1884 on how to divide up colonial possessions in Africa. Nicholas (1959: 19) argues that 'the idea of the Concert is to be found at the heart of the Charter', and the League Council and the UN Security Council represent the progression of this idea in the twentieth century, adding to it the principle of collective security and a permanent international organization.

The second influence is most visible at the Hague Peace Conferences of 1899 and 1907. These two gatherings represented the culmination of nineteenth-century efforts to promote the peaceful settlement of disputes and the regulation of warfare. Today these ideas are reflected in important aspects of the work of the International Court of Justice (ICJ) and in meetings about disarmament. Attendance at the two Hague Peace Conferences also demonstrated the widening of the international political system from its European core to embrace Asia (China, Japan, Siam) and Latin America (Archer, 1983: 8–9). This widening continued with the League, though only the UN has come close to being a truly global interstate body.

The third influence was on the economic, social and cultural work of the League and the UN. This can be traced back to the creation of specialized inter-governmental agencies to regulate waterways or provide important international services in an era of scientific progress that brought rapid improvements in communication and transportation. International commissions were created for the Elbe (1821), Rhine (1831) and Danube (1856). The first of the international service organizations was the International Telegraph Bureau, which was established in 1868. Other examples include the General Postal Union (1875), and the International Bureau of Weights and Measures (1875). In 1902 a Pan-American Sanitary Bureau was established in Washington and in 1909 the L'Office Internationale d'Hygiène Publique was set up in Paris. The 'Paris Office' was concerned with issues such as quarantinable diseases, the standardization of sera, and measures to stop the spread of venereal disease. The fact that these bodies had permanent secretariats allows us to view them as the forerunners of the functional agencies of the UN.

The legacy of the League

It was the League of Nations, created after the First World War to replace the discredited balance of power system with collective security, that had the most profound impact on the form that the UN was to take. The League should be viewed as not just the continuation of the trends noted in the previous section, for it was 'in some respects a radical departure' that depended on contingencies such as the Great War and the involvement of the US government in postwar reconstruction (Armstrong, Lloyd and Redmond, 1996: 7).

The basic structure of the League is remarkably similar to that of the UN. Its Council was transformed into the UN Security Council. The League Assembly, much more heterogeneous than the post-Napoleonic Concert system, became the General Assembly. The idea of an impartial international secretariat, one of the most innovative features of the League, was retained by the UN. The League was given responsibility for mandates: territories of the world such as Ruanda–Urundi, Palestine, Togoland, and some Pacific Islands were placed under the administration of the great powers, but were under League supervision. This idea was continued in the Trusteeship Council of the UN. So, as Nicholas (1959: 14) notes, 'in all the excitement that attended the accouchement of the new order, little attention had been paid to the obsequies of the old', though in practice the creators of the new organization 'paid the League a much more profound tribute than any formal eulogy could have expressed: they copied it'. The UN could, therefore, be described, with considerable justification, as a 'revised version of the League' (Claude, 1984: 60).

Yet lessons were also learnt from the failure of the League and there are some important differences between the two organizations. One of the lessons was that many felt 'that the reason for the League's failure lay not so much in the weakness of the Covenant's obligations, or the pusillanimity of its members, as in the deficiency of power available to it' (Luard, 1982: 6). So supporters of the United Nations attempted to ensure that the new international organization was equipped with a military capability that would provide the idea of collective security with a realistic means of implementation. This was something that the League clearly lacked, as demonstrated by the failures to stop Japanese aggression in Manchuria, the Italian invasion of Abyssinia, and Nazi territorial expansion in Central Europe.

The UN Charter was to ban the use of force in interstate relations, unless this was in self-defence or authorized by the Security Council. The League Covenant had never gone this far. The UN was also meant to have its own military force, made up of units provided by member states and under the control of a Military Staff Committee. This was an attempt to boost the credibility of collective security through more central control and it was not a feature of the League. Perhaps one of the most significant differences was that the UN abandoned the League's principle of unanimity, replacing it with a system of majority voting, but with the right of the permanent members of the Security Council to veto substantive decisions by this body.

The UN did not continue the League's system of minority protection (Ryan, 1990), but it put an emphasis on individual human rights that had not been found in the Covenant. There is also much greater emphasis in the UN Charter on the economic, social and cultural dimensions of peace. This emphasis was originally viewed by the US Secretary of State, Edward Stettinius, as a 'second front' to secure peace, but eventually these economic, social and cultural goals became ends in themselves (Sutterlin, 1995: 4).

The genesis of the United Nations

Another similarity between the League and the UN is that the US played the principal role in the creation of both organizations. President Franklin Roosevelt, who entered the White House in 1933, was personally committed to the idea of a new international organization to replace the discredited League, that had owed so much to the initial enthusiasm of President Woodrow Wilson. Roosevelt had been the Democratic nominee for vice-president in 1920 and made over eight hundred speeches in support of US membership of the League (Hoopes and Brinkley, 1997: 9). Then, during a period of illness in the 1920s, Roosevelt gave a lot of thought to how a new international organization could build on the League experience. In 1923 he had drawn up a detailed plan as a submission for the Edward Bok Peace Award. This was quite similar to the US draft for the UN put forward at the Dumbarton Oaks Conference 21 years later (Greer, 1958: 196), though some of the President's ideas were more radical than what eventually emerged in 1945. During the war, for example, Roosevelt had the idea that there should be a 'United Nations' news service that could disseminate accurate information through a number of 'free ports of information' around the world, and also suggested that the UN should control strategically located military bases (Sherwood, 1949, vol. 2: 705).

Like Woodrow Wilson, this wartime president also believed that the balance-of-power approach to international order was inadequate. In 1945 he informed Congress that the new international organization would be a substitute for the 'system of unilateral action, the exclusive alliances, the spheres of influence, the balances of power, and all the other expedients that have been tried for centuries and have always failed' (Thompson, 1978: 1). Real peace could only be achieved and guaranteed through an interstate organization that could speedily 'quarantine' aggressor nations (Greer, 1958: 196).

On 1 January 1942, less than four weeks after the US entry into the Second World War, 26 allied states issued the 'Declaration of the United Nations', drafted by the US State Department. This called for a new postwar system for general security and affirmed their commitment to the principles of the Atlantic Charter, the war aims agreed by Roosevelt and British Prime Minister Churchill after a meeting in Newfoundland in August 1941. An Advisory Committee on Postwar Foreign Policy was established with Secretary of State Cordell Hull as chairman and Under-Secretary Sumner Welles as vice-chairman. It first met on 12 February 1942, though most of the work on the future UN was conducted by a political sub-committee chaired by Welles.

The creation of what was to become the UN was not a foregone conclusion in 1942. The US still had to convince its two main allies to support the vision. Churchill was not attracted to the idea of a universal organization, pushing instead for a series of regional organizations in Europe, the Pacific and the Americas. He put these ideas to Roosevelt in his 'Morning Thoughts on Postwar Security' in February 1943. Churchill was sceptical of the idea of 'Big Four' collaboration and doubted whether China deserved equal status. Stalin, perpetually suspicious of the capitalist west and fearful that the proposed organization would be dominated by the US and its allies, could see few benefits in supporting Roosevelt's ideas. The USSR, it should be recalled, had not joined the League of Nations until 1934 and now displayed a much cooler attitude to the idea of the UN than did the US. Stalin continued to believe that the best way for the Soviet Union to protect its security was through its own military strength and an emphasis on the sovereignty and territorial integrity of his state.

Nevertheless, by March 1943 the Advisory Committee had produced a draft charter for the new organization, though according to Hull (1948: 1640) it was too regionalist in its proposals. In July 1943 the Secretary of State established a new drafting group for the United Nations Charter, which produced a 'tentative draft' in August which was more in line with Hull's universalistic inclinations. Suganami (1989: 122) has noted how these State Department officials involved in drafting the plans 'consistently referred to the League of Nations Covenant as a basis'. Planners were also influenced by several private organizations such as the Commission to Study the Organization of Peace and the Commission for a Just and Durable Peace (Bennett, 1995: 44–5).

In Moscow in October 1943, the foreign ministers of the 'Big Four' issued the 'Moscow Declaration of the Four Nations on General Security'. In this Declaration they did indeed agree that there would be a postwar international organization, global in its membership and based on the principle of sovereign equality. This was to be created at 'the earliest practicable date'. However, in addition, it was decided that the 'Big Three' would have a right to veto decisions of the new organization in the area of security matters. After the Moscow Conference Hull (1948: 1648) observed that 'we were now free to work wholeheartedly toward the single goal of establishing the United Nations organization'.

Roosevelt realised that the American public, and especially the Congress, would only support such an organization if Washington retained a right to veto enforcement action. The US Constitution gave the Senate the right to ratify the UN Charter as it was an international treaty, and it was this body's opposition to the Versailles settlement that had kept the US out of the League. Roosevelt and Hull were acutely aware that they had to maintain bipartisan support for the UN and both men worked hard to ensure this. Hull (1948: 1635), for example, ensured that 'the membership of the committee (on postwar foreign policy) was absolutely non-partisan' and that 'the mistakes made in 1919–20, which led to the United States holding aloof from the League of Nations, should not recur'. The policy bore fruit when both the Senate and the House of Representatives passed resolutions supporting US participation in a postwar security system. The Fulbright Resolution in the House was passed on 21 September 1943 'favoring the creation of appropriate international machinery with power adequate to establish and maintain a just and lasting peace'. The Senate's Connolly Resolution on November 5 stated that the US should 'join with free and sovereign nations in the establishment and maintenance of international authority with power to prevent aggression and to preserve the peace of the world'. Another benefit of the administration's bipartisan policy was that the issue of the UN was kept out of the 1944 US Presidential election campaign and the country did not split on US participation in the new organization in the way that it had over League membership during the presidential campaign of 1920.

The support of the Soviet Union and the UK could only be obtained by extending the veto right to Moscow and London. One of the major flaws of the League was that not all the great powers were members, fatally undermining the principle of collective security. The veto was the price that had to be paid to ensure that all of the three wartime allies joined the new organization. The irony was that this concession made collective action by the Security Council impossible once the Cold War started and wartime partners became adversaries.

Serious, high-level inter-governmental debate about the actual structure of the UN began in 1943 at the 'Big Three' conference in Tehran. In a bilateral meeting at this conference Roosevelt presented his views to Stalin. The postwar organization, he proposed, should be made up of three main organs. A world-wide General Assembly would be made up of the states of the world. An Executive Committee would be created to provide advice on non-military questions and would be composed of the four big powers (US, USSR, UK and China) and states appointed to represent regions. Finally, and most importantly, there would be an 'enforcement agency' made up of the 'Big Four'. Roosevelt's thinking was based on the idea that the big powers on the allied side could play the role of 'world policemen'. His original plan was that these 'policemen' would guarantee international peace for several years after the end of the war until the new organization was created. But at Tehran it seems that the 'policeman' idea had become the bedrock of the new organization.

At Tehran Roosevelt also presented a sketchy outline of the UN in the form of a diagram:

> Some time during the Teheran Conference Roosevelt drew three circles, which represented his conception of the basis of the United Nations Organization. The centre circle was marked 'Executive Committee', the one on the right was marked '4 Policemen', and the one on the left '40 United Nations' (The General Assembly), under which came the 'I.L.O.–Health–Agriculture–Food'. (Sherwood, 1949, vol. 2: 784)

At their bilateral meeting Stalin responded that the smaller European states would be unhappy with the four policemen idea and he pointed out that China was not strong enough to be included as a big power. Then, like Churchill, he went on to propose the idea of regional organizations in Europe and the Far East. Roosevelt replied that the Congress would not allow him to give US military backing to such regional bodies. No firm decisions were made.

In July 1944 the Bretton Woods Conference in Washington established the principal organizations of the postwar economic order. These reflected the US emphasis on economic liberalism and free trade. The International Bank for Reconstruction and Development (usually referred to as the World Bank) was established to provide capital for a wide range of projects. Its main purpose in the immediate postwar world was to assist the reconstruction of Europe. The International Monetary Fund (IMF) was meant to be the cornerstone of the postwar international financial system, based on fixed exchange rates. An attempt to establish a third Bretton Woods institution – the International Trade Organization – to reduce barriers to international trade could not muster enough support. However, its role was eventually taken up by the General Agreement on Tariffs and Trade (GATT).

Other components of what was to become known as the UN system had also been established before the final shape of the organization was decided. The United Nations Relief and Rehabilitation Administration (UNRAA) and the Food and Agriculture Organization (FAO) had both been created in 1943. The latter organization met for the first time in Quebec in October 1945 under the leadership of the Scottish academic Boyd-Orr. His work for this specialised agency was recognised in 1949 when he was awarded the Nobel Peace Prize. A new International Civil Aviation Organization was set up in 1944.

The creation of the postwar security system took a major step forward at the Dumbarton Oaks Conference in Washington in August 1944. Here, the principal features of the United Nations were worked out. The conference was held in two stages, because the USSR had not yet declared war on Japan and was therefore a neutral country in the Pacific War. So first the US, UK and the USSR and then the US, UK and China agreed a working document, the 'Proposals for the Establishment of a General International Organization'. This was based on the US draft which had been circulated to the other participants in advance. So, as we have already noted, the League Council became the UN Security Council, the Assembly became the General Assembly, the Permanent Court of International Justice the International Court of Justice, and the idea of a permanent international secretariat was retained. Therefore, as Fehrenbach (1967: 21) points out, 'the lights burning late at Dumbarton Oaks were not beacons illuminating a coming millennium or a brave new world in which all the old rules were changed.'

The plans for the United Nations (the name was accepted by the 'Big Four' shortly after the conference ended) agreed at

Dumbarton Oaks meant that France was now included as a permanent member of the proposed Security Council. An American idea that Brazil should also be granted similar status was emphatically rejected by London and Moscow. However, although the basic shape of the UN was now clear some issues could not be resolved at Dumbarton Oaks and had to be addressed at the next meeting involving the leaders of the 'Big Three', which took place in Yalta in February 1945.

Although the US, the USSR and the UK had already agreed on the principle of the veto there was still a disagreement about when it could be used. The Soviet Union, fearing that the UN could legitimize external intervention in its internal affairs, insisted that the veto could be used even if the vetoing state was a party to the dispute. This was not acceptable to the US or the UK. Eventually a compromise was reached whereby a veto could be exercised by a party to a dispute, but only to prevent enforcement action. It could not be used to stop the Security Council discussing a dispute. Another issue discussed at Yalta was the number of representatives in the General Assembly allocated to the territories of the USSR. In addition to a seat for the USSR, Stalin wanted separate accreditation for the Ukraine and Byelorussia, which was itself a weakening of his original idea, tabled at Dumbarton Oaks, that all 15 of the Soviet republics should have their own representation. The US had made it clear that they totally opposed the idea of the 15 republics all obtaining seats at the UN, but there was agreement that the Ukraine and Byelorussia should become 'independent' members of the new organization.

The conference also agreed a trusteeship role for the UN, an issue not discussed at Dumbarton Oaks. Under this system the UN would take responsibility for certain territories. Three sources of trusteeship status were identified: the former League mandates such as Palestine, Tanganyika, Western Samoa and Ruanda–Urundi; territory detached from the Axis powers during the Second World War, for example, Italian Somaliland or some of the Pacific Island groups captured from the

Japanese; and finally, it was envisaged that territories could voluntarily be placed under UN trusteeship.

Tremors at San Francisco

At San Francisco the 'Big Four' presented their agreed working draft of the UN to other governments, who were allowed to attend if they had either signed the 1942 Declaration of the United Nations or had declared war on the Axis powers before March 1945. France was invited to be a fifth sponsoring state by the 'Big Four', but declined because de Gaulle objected to the fact that it had been excluded from the drafting process. In all, 50 states attended, including Byelorussia and Ukraine. The fact that the Soviet Foreign Minister Molotov did not attend the conference has generally been taken to be an indication of the unimportance that the Kremlin attached to the meeting.

Roosevelt did not live to witness the birth of the organization he had championed. He died of a cerebral haemorrhage on 12 April and was replaced by his vice-president, Harry S. Truman. Hull had also resigned as Secretary of State, though he was awarded the Nobel Peace Prize in 1945 in recognition of his contribution to the establishment of the UN. Truman's first decision as the new president was to confirm that the San Francisco Conference would go ahead as planned (Simons, 1994: 44). The conference opened in the city's opera house on 25 April, on the day that Soviet forces completed their encirclement of Berlin, and it continued to meet through the final defeat of Germany. Nicholas (1959: 9) points out that this gave the participants at the conference an 'almost constant awareness of the pressure of history'. It has been claimed that San Francisco was an appropriate venue because, like the United Nations, it rests on a permanent fault. Furthermore, given the theatrical nature of the meetings, an opera house was not an inappropriate location. Many of the sessions took place in front of the world's press in a room where four columns representing the four freedoms of the Atlantic Charter rose from the floor, and delegates sat in striking red seats (Simons, 1994: 44). The set was designed by a Broadway specialist, Jo Mielziner, who interrupted work on a play to perform this task for the government. The play was called 'Foolish Notion' (Melvern, 1995: 23). The sense of drama was increased because decisions at the conference were taken by a two-thirds majority, with each amendment voted on clause by clause.

There was also drama off-stage. Many of the smaller powers were not happy with the 'Big Four' proposals and sought changes. The criticisms concentrated on three main issues: the relative weakness of the General Assembly compared with the Security Council; the nature of representation on the Security Council and the privileged position given to the permanent members; and the lack of clarity about the use of the veto by these permanent members. This last worry, which caused the most significant debate at San Francisco, prompted the smaller states to send a 23-part questionnaire to the sponsoring powers. Although they did not reply to each point raised, the 'Big Four' did issue a 'Statement by the Delegates of the Four Sponsoring Governments on Voting Procedures on the Security Council', which became known as the San Francisco Statement. This listed the items that were to be considered procedural rather than substantive, and therefore not subject to the veto. However, the statement also made plain that any disagreement about whether an issue was procedural or substantive would itself be a substantive matter. This gave rise to what was known as the 'double veto'. The Soviet delegation, never happy with any restrictions at all on the use of the veto, was to make significant use of this double veto provision during the Cold War (Bailey, 1969).

The questionnaire also exposed an underlying conflict between the US and Soviet delegations about how to interpret the Yalta agreement on the use of the veto. This was only resolved when Harry Hopkins, one of Roosevelt's closest advisors, met with Stalin on a mission to Moscow. Stalin seemed to be uninformed about this conflict, which could have wrecked the San Francisco Conference (Hoopes and Brinkley,

1997: 200–1). When he was told what was happening the Soviet leader considered the matter to be unimportant and ordered Molotov to accept the US interpretation. This meant that no permanent member of the Security Council could use its veto to stop the Council considering an issue.

The great powers had a common interest in defending their special status, and were able to resist major changes to the Dumbarton Oaks draft. Nonetheless, as Goodwin (1957: 27) notes, the submission of a postwar peace plan to a representative international gathering had never happened before; neither at 'Vienna nor at Versailles had the smaller states been treated with such consideration'. As a result these smaller states were able to influence the shape of the UN and although the 'Big Four' opposed any major alterations to their working document, some amendments were successfully proposed by other states.

The section on regional organizations (Chapter VIII) was strengthened and Article 51 of the Charter was amended to include the right of collective self defence. Canadian efforts ensured that if a country not on the Security Council contributed troops to enforce international peace and security it would be entitled to participate in Security Council discussions and vote on the use of its forces (Article 44). The Economic, Social and Cultural Organization (ECOSOC) was made a principal organ (Chapter X) and the Trusteeship Council was established as another principal organ. The General Assembly was given the right to 'discuss any questions or any other matters within the scope of the present Charter or relating to the powers and functions of any organs provided for in the present Charter' (Article 10). Although this left the power of the Security Council intact, it also enhanced the role of the General Assembly. When the USSR proposed that the term of office for the Secretary-General should be restricted to two years without an opportunity for re-selection, thus limiting the power of the office, it was the smaller states who led the resistance to this idea. Human rights received more attention in the Charter because of lobbying by these smaller states and they were also able to incorporate a 'Declaration Regarding Non-Self-Governing Territories' as Chapter XI of the Charter.

The Conference ended on 26 June, when 51 states signed the UN Charter. Poland had not been represented at San Francisco, but did become one of the original signatories. Eight days later the US became the first state to ratify the Charter. When all the permanent members of the Security Council and the majority of all signatories had completed the ratification process the Charter came into force. This occurred on 24 October 1945. In November 1945 a Preparatory Commission made up of all member states met in London to draft rules of procedure and provisional agendas for the various bodies and to agree on the nature of the Secretariat.

The structure of the United Nations

The basic structure of the UN is clearly set out in the Charter. There are six principal organs: the General Assembly, the Security Council, the Secretariat, ECOSOC, the Trusteeship Council and the ICJ. Many additional specialized agencies orbit around these central bodies.

The Assembly, in which every member state has one vote, meets in regular session for a three-month period every year. This starts on the third Tuesday of September with a 'general debate' where representatives of states (often heads of government) make speeches on topics that are of particular concern to them. Nicholas (1959: 97) cynically points out that 'anything less like a debate could hardly be imagined, though its generality is indubitable.'

On important issues such as membership and peace and security the General Assembly makes decisions by a two-thirds majority of members present and voting. Other decisions are made by a simple majority. It is allowed to initiate studies, discuss issues, consider reports from other UN bodies and make recommendations on a wide range of topics. However, it cannot discuss peace and security issues if an issue that comes under this heading is already being considered by the Security Council and, unlike the Security Council, it cannot pass legally binding resolutions. So although it has a 'parliamentary' style of debate, it lacks the most crucial feature of national legislatures. It also approves the UN's budget and apportions the contributions among its members.

The General Assembly has seven main committees, where most of the work is actually done: the Political and Security Committee; the Economic and Financial Committee; the Social, Humanitarian and Cultural Committee; the Trusteeship Committee; the Administrative and Budgetary Committee; the Legal Committee; and the Special Political Committee. There is also a General Committee and a Credentials Committee. The Assembly has created many more specialized committees, such as the Committee on the Peaceful Uses of Outer Space, the Temporary Commission on Korea, the Commission on Atomic Energy, and the Special Committee on Peacekeeping Operations. Outside its annual meeting the Assembly, using Article 20 of the Charter, can call special sessions. These have been convened to debate a number of topics, including the future of Palestine (1947–8), disarmament (1978 and 1988), economic development (1975), Namibia (1978), and the international drugs problem (1990).

Nicholas (1959: Ch. 5) has argued that the General Assembly has five main functions. First, it is an arena for debate, reflecting the views and interests of all regions of the globe. Second, it has a quasi-legal role in that its activities can contribute to the development of international law (Article 13). For although the General Assembly cannot pass legally binding resolutions, these can be taken to be evidence of customary international law. To help it in its efforts to encourage the progressive development and the codification of international law the General Assembly established the International Law Commission in 1948. Third, it is an organ of political settlement and peacemaking. As we shall see, the General Assembly has established peacekeeping forces and its deliberations have also played a significant role in some conflicts. Fourth, it supervises the work of other UN bodies such as ECOSOC, the Trusteeship Council and the Secretariat and reviews annual reports from all of these bodies. Finally, it has an electoral role, deciding who will fill the vacant government seats on the Security Council, ECOSOC and the Trusteeship Council. It also appoints the Secretary-General on the recommendation of the Security Council, and the Assembly and the Council are jointly responsible for appointing the judges of the International Court of Justice.

The Security Council has primary responsibility for international peace and security, and can make decisions in this field that states are obliged to act on (Article 24). This does not mean that all Security Council decisions are binding, for it can also pass resolutions that just 'request' or 'call upon' states to do certain things. Unlike the General Assembly it has no fixed meeting times and a session can be convened at short notice. Indeed, it has to be organized so that it can 'function continuously' (Article 28).

The Council was originally composed of the five permanent members (US, USSR, UK, France and China), all of whom have the power of veto on substantive issues, and six non-permanent members. The number of non-permanent members was raised to ten in 1965. These non-permanent members are elected by a two-thirds majority of the General Assembly to serve for a two-year term. These states are chosen according to geographical quotas. Non-members can be invited to participate in Security Council discussions, but they are not allowed to vote. The presidency of the Security Council rotates every month and it operates in six languages: English, French, Chinese, Russian, Spanish and Arabic.

It can establish any subsidiary bodies that it deems necessary. Early examples of these included a Committee on Admission of New Members (1946), the Commission for Conventional Armaments (1947), the Committee of Good Offices on the Indonesian Question (1947), and the Select Committee on the Palestinian Question (1948). More recent examples include the United Nations Special Commission

(UNSCOM) that is attempting to monitor Iraqi compliance with UN resolutions demanding that it destroy weapons of mass destruction, and a Compensation Commission that was given the task of examining claims for compensation against Iraq that arose from Iraq's invasion of Kuwait.

The Secretariat is the administrative organ of the UN. It is headed by the UN Secretary-General, described in Article 97 as the chief administrative officer of the organization. He is appointed by a two-thirds vote in the General Assembly on the recommendation of the Security Council. This ensures that he will not be opposed, at least at first, by any of the 'Big Five'. However, even if he does upset some of the influential UN members he cannot be dismissed by them once appointed, and serves a fixed term, though its exact length is not specified in the Charter. His main function is to serve, and implement the decisions of, the UN bodies. However, Article 99 of the Charter gives the Secretary-General a more political role, allowing him to bring to the attention of the Security Council any matter which could be a threat to international peace and security. This makes the Secretary-General more than just an administrator and allows him to raise substantive political issues. As Ford (1957: 84–5) notes, the 'extraordinary possibilities that could result from a broad interpretation of these powers to investigate and report are sufficiently obvious as to need no elaboration.'

There is an obvious tension between the Secretary-General's role as servant of other bodies and his role as an initiator of UN action. This has frequently caused antagonism with the Security Council. Skjelsbaek and Fermann (1996: 88) claim that the 'major powers may delegate tasks to the Secretary-General, but in general they do not want him to exercise leadership.' Successive Secretaries-General have incurred the wrath of one or other of the permanent members when they are perceived to be playing an active role against that state's interests – for they usually want him to be more Secretary than General.

The Secretary-General also has the right to attend, and participate in, the meetings of the General Assembly, the Security Council, ECOSOC and the Trusteeship Council (Article 98), and it has become the practice that he can place an item on the draft agendas of the Assembly and the three Councils. The Secretary-General also prepares the provisional budget of the UN, collects contributions from member states, recruits the Secretariat staff and determines their conditions of employment.

About 13 000 members of the UN Secretariat work at the UN headquarters in New York, though the entire UN system, including the specialized agencies, employs about 51 000 people (Whittaker, 1995: 19). In 1945 it was decided to divide the Secretariat into eight departments: Security Council Affairs, Economic Affairs, Social Affairs, Trusteeship and Information from Non Self-Governing Territories, Legal, Public Information, Administration and Financial Services, and Conference and General Services. Each would be headed by an Assistant Secretary-General. The Secretariat staff who serve in these departments under the Secretary-General are supposed to give their primary loyalty to the organization, not to the states they are nationals of. Article 100 states that the Secretary-General and his staff should not 'seek or receive instructions from any governments or from any authority external to the organization'.

The Secretary-General is free to choose his own Secretariat staff, but in practice considerable pressure can be applied by the larger powers to ensure certain appointments. In addition the freedom of appointment is restricted because posts in the Secretariat are subject to a system of regional quotas, which can mean that the most talented people do not always reach top positions. Each state is allocated a 'desirable range' for the number of its nationals employed by the UN. In 1993, for example, the quota for British citizens was set between 70 and 94 (Bailey and Daws, 1995: 28). These quotas have been applied despite the fact that, although Article 101 of the

Charter states that due regard should be paid to the importance of recruiting staff from as wide a geographical basis as
possible, the 'paramount consideration in the employment of
the staff and in the determination of the conditions of service
shall be the necessity of securing the highest standards of
efficiency, competence and integrity.' It is interesting to note
that in the early years of the UN the USSR never achieved its
quota. Dallin (1962: 101) reveals that in 1955 its quota was
131–75, but there were only 19 Soviet citizens on the staff of
the Secretariat.

It became the practice to allocate specific senior posts to the
nationals of Permanent Members of the Security Council.
Thus the Assistant Secretary-General for Economic Affairs
was a UK national, a Soviet citizen would be the Assistant
Secretary-General for Political and Security Council Affairs,
and an American would expect to be the Assistant Secretary-
General for Administrative and Financial Affairs. Ford (1957:
95–6) points out that: 'Any Assistant Secretaries who act as the
appointees of national states are not likely to be persons in
whom the Secretary-General can have complete trust and
confidence.' However, each Secretary-General developed his
own mechanisms to ensure that these problems did not unduly
affect his freedom of action (Bennett, 1995: 419).

The Secretariat has been reorganized several times since
1945. At the time of writing it was composed of the following
departments and offices: the Executive Office of the Secretary-
General; the Office of Internal Oversight Services; the Department of Political Affairs; the Department of Peacekeeping
Operations; the Department of Humanitarian Affairs; the
Department of Policy Coordination and Sustainable Development; the Department for Economic and Social Information
and Policy Analysis; the Department for Development Support and Management Services; the Department of Public
Information; and the Department of Administration and
Management. All of these are based in New York. In addition
there are the UN offices away from UN headquarters, in
Geneva and Vienna. This does not take into account the

various specialized agencies and regional commissions which are located at various places around the world.

ECOSOC is the principal organ of the UN most directly involved in the fields of economic development, social progress, human rights, inter-cultural understanding and health and welfare. It is meant to: promote higher standards of living, full employment, economic and social progress; solve international economic, health and related problems; and promote universal respect for the observance of human rights and fundamental freedoms. According to Article 62 of the Charter it can make or initiate studies and reports and produce recommendations in these areas. These can eventually be turned into UN Conventions. ECOSOC was originally composed of 18 members, though this was increased to 27 in 1965 and to 54 in 1973. States serve three-year terms and they are elected by the General Assembly. Although the Charter makes no mention of permanent members it has become customary for the 'Big Five' to be elected on a 'quasi-permanent' basis through repeated re-selection. Each ECOSOC member has one vote and decisions are made by simple majority. It holds an annual meeting for five to six weeks in either New York or Geneva.

ECOSOC has no direct control over the UN specialized agencies such as UNESCO, the World Health Organization (WHO), the FAO and so on. Many of these have their own constitution and their membership may not be the same as that of the UN. An administrative Committee on Coordination was established under the chairmanship of the Secretary-General to conduct meetings between the heads of these specialized agencies. These occur about three times a year. However, ECOSOC is authorized by the Charter to obtain regular reports from these agencies.

ECOSOC itself has also become a 'residuary legatee', taking responsibility for economic, social and cultural issues in areas where no specialized agency exists (Lewis, 1957). To this end it has created a number of functional commissions on topics such as human rights, the status of women, population and development, transnational corporations, sustainable development and narcotic drugs. Although these commissions could have been composed of independent experts in their fields, the UN decided that they should be composed of government delegations. Some commentators feel that this has had a destructive impact on the work of these commissions, because of the 'politicization' that accompanies the governmental perspective (Nicholas, 1959: 124). ECOSOC has also established regional economic commissions in Africa (ECA), Europe (ECE), Latin America (ECLA), Asia and the Pacific (ECAP) and West Asia (ECWA). These provide forums where states can discuss regional economic issues and they also publish authoritative reports on matters under their remit. Over 600 non-governmental organizations have consultative status with the Council.

The ICJ is the principal judicial organ of the UN (Article 92) and all members of the UN are *ipso facto* parties to the ICJ Statute (Article 93). It has no automatic right of jurisdiction because states must agree to submit a dispute to the Court, which cannot compel governments to attend. One way states can accept the jurisdiction of the Court is by signing the 'optional clause', which is found in Article 36 of the Court's Statute. By this article states can declare that they accept the compulsory jurisdiction of the Court, but they usually add reservations to such an acceptance. About one-third of all states have signed the optional clause, many with important reservations attached. The US, for example, has signed the 'optional clause' but refuses the Court jurisdiction over disputes within its domestic jurisdiction, as determined by the United States. Many international treaties also contain articles declaring that if there is a dispute about the treaty it will be submitted to the ICJ. Only states can be parties to litigation.

The Court has 15 independent judges, who enjoy diplomatic immunities and privileges. They are elected for nine years by the Assembly and the Council, and no state is allowed more than one judge. In addition, if a state before the Court does not have a judge who is a citizen of that state already on the Court it can appoint one on an *ad hoc* basis for that case only.

It can make two types of judgements. Judicial decisions are legally binding on states and are made to resolve a particular case before the court. Advisory opinions are made at the request of the General Assembly, the Security Council, or any other organ of the UN. They clarify a point of international law.

The Trusteeship Council, like ECOSOC, is under the authority of the General Assembly. It was created to supervise the trust territories for which the UN had responsibility. Countries responsible for administrating the trust territories were obliged to ensure 'the economic, social, and educational advancement of the inhabitants of the trust territories, and their progressive development towards self-government or independence' (Article 76). The Council was also able to receive petitions from these territories and to make visits there. Administering states had to respond on an annual basis to a questionnaire drafted by the Trusteeship Council. There were 11 trust territories established: Cameroon, Ruanda-Urundi, Somaliland, Togoland, Tanganyika, Western Samoa, the Pacific Islands (Marianas, Marshalls and the Carolines), New Guinea and Nauru. All but Somaliland had been League of Nations mandates. By 1962 eight of these 11 had attained self-rule (Bennett, 1995: 385).

In order to satisfy US security concerns the Trust Territory of the Pacific Islands, formerly under Japanese control and now allocated to the US itself, was declared a strategic area. This meant that in theory the Security Council, not the General Assembly, would take over the functions and responsibilities of the United Nations for this territory. In practice, the US was able to use the strategic area designation to sidestep criticisms made of the way it administered some of these Pacific islands, most notably Bikini Atoll, which was turned into a military area for the testing of American nuclear weapons. In October 1994 Palau, the last Trusteeship, obtained its independence. The next month the Trusteeship Council suspended operation and will now meet as occasions require. It has abandoned its annual meetings.

From the Opera House to the Slaughterhouse

The Preparatory Commission of the United Nations also discussed the location of the UN. Roosevelt thought that the UN could be located at a number of sites around the globe (Hull, 1948: 1681–2). The Secretariat could be based in Geneva; the General Assembly could meet in a different city every year; and the Security Council could have two meeting places. There would be an Atlantic site in the Azores and a Pacific location in Hawaii. It is clear, however, that the US government never took these suggestions seriously and they were not raised at international meetings to discuss the UN.

There was disagreement between many European states, who wanted a European site (Geneva, The Hague, Vienna and Prague were all mentioned), and other states, including the USSR, who preferred to locate the new organization in the US. The USSR, however, objected to a west-coast site. The Commission eventually decided on a site on the east coast of the US and a seven-member group was sent to inspect locations in North Stamford and the Greenwich areas of Connecticut. However they ran into local opposition at every site examined.

A decision was only made to locate the permanent headquarters in New York City when, on 11 December 1946, John D. Rockefeller Jr. gave the Organization $8.5 million to purchase an area of land called 'Turtle Bay' along the East River in mid-town Manhattan, part of which was the site of a former slaughterhouse. The US government also provided an interest-free loan of $65 million to help with the construction of the new headquarters on this site. This was built with the expectation that it would have to house, at most, 90 delegations (Fetherston, 1994: 9).

Until the headquarters was built the UN had a peripatetic existence. The first meeting of the General Assembly, for example, took place in London from 10 January 1946. It then moved to a converted skating rink in Flushing. The Secretariat found temporary headquarters at Hunter College in the Bronx and then at Lake Success in Long Island. The headquarters building was completed in October 1952. By then the role that the UN was to play in international politics had become clearer.

2

PARALYSIS? THE UN AND THE COLD WAR

The United Nations of the Charter is a ruin, rent asunder by the conflict between East and West. (Morgenthau, 1967: 480)

It should be clear from the previous chapter that the main function of the UN, as conceived by the wartime allies, was to promote international peace and security. States that signed the Charter were committing themselves to Article 2(4), which required them to refrain from the use of force or the threat of the use of force in their relations with one another, except in self-defence or where the Security Council deemed there to be a threat to international peace and security. Aggression would be deterred and the status quo maintained by collective security, which progressive writers saw as the alternative to the balance-of-power system that, it was argued, had been discredited by the First World War. As Claude (1984: 245) points out, the concept of collective security, which has had a central place in orthodox thinking about international organizations in this century, epitomised the idea that such bodies should prevent war or defend states subjected to armed attack.

Claude (1984: Ch. 12) also argues that such a security system could only work if certain preconditions were in place.

Any commitment to protect the interest of the world community of states had to be seen as being compatible with the national interest of these states. States had to accept both the idea of the 'indivisibility of peace' and a commitment to uphold this idea, irrespective of the costs involved. In other words, states had to be willing to fight against an aggressor anywhere and at any time and this had to have priority over any bilateral or regional security arrangements agreed to by states. Thus all victims should be equally important (Weiss, Forsyth and Coate, 1994: 23). It should also be clear that if collective security is to be effective then those states fighting for the status quo had to have the resources to defeat an aggressor. Furthermore, the deterrent effect of a collective security system would only work if the margin of military superiority was very wide. So it is usually accepted that all the great powers should be on the side of the collective security system to allow it to deter possible aggressors. Claude's final criterion is that the collective security apparatus has to be such that it can be implemented smoothly and cannot be stalled or derailed by any state or group of states who want to block it in any particular case.

One other important precondition is that there has to be agreement about what counts as an aggressive act. Although this may appear to be a straightforward matter, in practice it has not always been easy for the international community to reach consensus about when violence is legitimate. The UN began its attempts to define 'aggression' at the San Francisco Conference, but it was only in 1974 that the General Assembly accepted a vague definition which was meant to guide discussions in the Security Council. The problem is that 'what is aggression for one is self-defence for another and national liberation for a third'(Eban, 1995: 46). Even if an acceptable definition can be found, the facts of particular acts of aggression are not always clear enough to allow the UN to apportion blame in a non-controversial way.

This chapter will examine how the UN's collective security mechanism was supposed to work. It will also point out how it failed to meet the criteria for a viable mechanism because of superpower rivalry. This, in turn, resulted in a fundamental failure of the organization in what should have been its main function almost immediately after it was created.

The collective security provisions of the Charter

The Security Council was created to be the principal organ for protecting international peace and security and was given powers to make decisions in this field that are legally binding on member states. The collective security provisions are found in the 13 articles that make up Chapter VII of the Charter. The first of these, Article 39, makes it clear that the Security Council 'shall determine the existence of any threat to the peace, breach of the peace, or act of aggression and shall make recommendations, or decide what measures shall be taken in accordance with Articles 41 and 42'. These two articles allow the Council to decide what measures should be taken. Article 41 refers to actions 'not involving the use of armed force', such as the interruption of economic relations or the severance of diplomatic relations. This article was only invoked in two cases during the Cold War. In 1966 partial economic sanctions were imposed against the white minority government in Rhodesia after the Smith regime declared its independence from Britain in order to maintain a quasi-apartheid system. In 1968 these partial sanctions were made comprehensive, though they were never implemented successfully, for trade with Rhodesia continued with the help of South Africa and the Portuguese colony of Mozambique, and western governments turned a blind eye to breaches of the sanctions. In 1977 the Security Council also imposed a mandatory arms embargo against South Africa, but was unable to agree on comprehensive economic sanctions.

Article 42 enables the Council to take such military action 'as may be necessary to maintain or restore international peace and security'. To facilitate military action it was envisaged that all members of the UN would negotiate agreements with the Security Council that would set out the numbers and types of forces and facilities that they would make available (Article 43). The Security Council would determine what action to take and which states would be involved (Article 48). In order to make possible urgent military action Article 45 states that member states would 'hold immediately available national air-force contingents for combined international enforcement action'. A Military Staff Committee was created by Article 47, composed of military experts from the five permanent members (the Chiefs of Staff or their representatives), to advise and assist the Security Council on military matters and to give 'strategic direction' to military action. The issue of who would actually command such action is left open. Finally, until the Security Council was able to take measures to maintain international peace and security, Article 51 allows states to retain the right of individual or collective self-defence.

The Charter, therefore, appears to give the Security Council considerable legal authority and military capability. James (1987: 214) claims that 'the United Nations Charter undoubtedly provided, on paper, a strong system for the maintenance of peace.' In practice, however, the collective security provisions, with one or two exceptions, remained unused because of the onset of the Cold War. It is to this we can now turn.

The impact of the Cold War

The hopes for a strong postwar international organization rested on the continuation of 'big five' co-operation after the defeat of Germany and Japan removed their need for an anti-Fascist alliance. However a series of incidents in Europe and Asia between 1945 and the end of the decade made it clear that not only was it impossible to maintain good relations between the US and the USSR but also the UN, except at the margins, could play no significant role in regulating or restraining the Cold War that developed between them.

Already, at the San Francisco Conference, the voting record revealed a growing divergence between the two blocs about the role of the UN (Nicholas, 1959: 9). Moscow also protested about the invitation extended to pro-Fascist Argentina to become one of the original members. The clashes continued at the very first Security Council meeting, held in London on 19 January 1946. Here consideration was given to a claim from Iran that Moscow was supporting an Azerbaijan secessionist movement on Iranian territory. This developed into the first major public breach between the two superpowers. Two days later the Council heard a complaint from the Soviet delegate about British interference in Greece, and the Ukraine condemned the British for their suppression of independence movements in the Dutch East Indies. Trygve Lie (1954: 32), the newly appointed Secretary-General, was 'deeply shocked by the bitterness of the debate'.

The Iranian issue resurfaced on 18 March when Iran, with the support of Washington, complained to the Security Council that Soviet troops, who had occupied parts of this state during the Second World War to protect the Iranian oil fields, had not been withdrawn. According to a Tripartite Agreement between Iran, the USSR and the UK, British and Soviet forces would leave Iran within six months of the end of the war. Lie (1954: 76) noted the 'dramatic lessons' offered by the ensuing Security Council debate. The Soviet representative requested a postponement of debate to give him time to prepare his case. When this was not granted he walked out of the meeting. When he returned to the Security Council he demanded that the issue should be removed from the agenda entirely, since during his absence Iran, anxious not to provoke its powerful neighbour, had agreed not to press for a debate if the USSR withdrew its troops within six weeks. However, other Security Council members decided, against the view of the Secretary-General, that the matter would simply be deferred. Luard (1982: 115) has concluded that nobody 'can be certain that events in the Council had the smallest influence on Soviet actions', but that the discussions at the UN probably 'did have the effect of magnifying the pressure of outside opinion on the Soviet Union'.

The Cold War also doomed the efforts of the Military Staff Committee to reach a consensus on how to implement Article 43, which relates to agreements between the Security Council and states for the provision of military forces for UN operations. After working for a year the Committee had to report that there were strong disagreements on matters such as the size of forces (the US wanted a large force of 20 divisions, 4000 aircraft and a large navy, the other permanent members wished for a much smaller one); the extent of individual contributions (the US wanted flexibility, the USSR insisted on strict equality); and the location of these forces in peace time (the USSR wanted them to remain in their own states, the others wanted them to be deployed at the discretion of the Security Council). China and France wanted the right to withdraw contingents from collective action on grounds of national emergency, but this was opposed by the other three. With a divided Security Council unable to provide any guidance to it, the Military Staff Committee decided that no further progress could be made. So the legal agreements with states which were needed to allow the Security Council to order military action were never signed. Henceforth the Council, as in the case of Korea, could only recommend military action to member states.

The Baruch Plan

The delegates who finalised the content of the UN Charter did not know that nuclear weapons existed (Eban, 1995: 43–4). But on the same day in 1945 that the San Francisco Conference opened the newly installed President Truman was given a memorandum by the Secretary of War that pointed out that nuclear proliferation was inevitable and that no known system of control could cope with this (Donovan, 1977: 10). In response the President established an Interim

Committee to investigate future nuclear arms policy. This recommended that atomic weapons should be used against Japan and that the USSR should be informed about the weapon before it was used. America's hopes for future talks on nuclear policy should also be conveyed to Stalin. In the event Truman simply told Stalin at the Potsdam Conference that the US had developed a powerful weapon that they thought would end the war. No mention was made of atomic power or of possible future discussions.

In January 1946 the General Assembly created an Atomic Energy Commission, which became the location of one of the most remarkable initiatives in the early history of the UN. At the first meeting of this Commission, in June 1946 at Hunter College in New York, an American proposal was tabled. Known as the Baruch Plan (after the head of the US delegation, Bernard Baruch), or the Acheson–Lilienthal plan (after the two people who led the committee that drafted it), it suggested that an Atomic Energy Authority should be created to take over the ownership of nuclear materials and the control and licensing of atomic facilities in all states. It would also promote the peaceful uses of nuclear energy and provide member states with security against attack from any state that had illegally developed nuclear weapons. An intrusive inspection system would enable the Authority to detect such states and the proposed agency would also be provided with enforcement capabilities. The US government also declared that it would dispose of its own nuclear weapons when the Authority had demonstrated its effectiveness and the Authority would be given all the information the US had gathered on atomic energy.

However, the Soviet Union was suspicious. If the American plan was implemented it would be much harder, if not impossible, for its own scientists to advance their own understanding of the military and civilian uses of nuclear power. The US had already accumulated this knowledge. The Baruch Plan would also move forward in stages. A survey of atomic facilities and raw materials would come before any surrender of weapons. So the USSR would have to provide information on its own nuclear programmes before the US had to hand over its nuclear arsenal. Furthermore, in 1946 the UN was dominated by allies of the US. Only five states were communist out of a total membership of 51. Could the Soviet Union, therefore, accept that the proposed UN Atomic Energy Authority would operate in a neutral manner rather than reflect US interests? Anyway, Moscow seemed opposed in principle to extending the powers of the UN over states, and the intrusive powers of the Authority went against Stalin's strong attachment to the sovereignty and independence of the USSR. Therefore, the Soviet diplomat Gromyko responded to the Baruch plan by pointing out that

> When the Charter of the United Nations was prepared . . . the question of sovereignty was one of the most important questions considered. This principle of sovereignty is one of the cornerstones on which the United Nations structure is built; if this were breached the whole existence and future of the United Nations would be threatened. (in Schell, 1984: 42)

So the USSR put forward a counter-proposal. This would have drastically reduced the Authority's powers of control and supervision and it would be under the Security Council, where the veto could be used to protect the interests of permanent members. The Soviet proposals also insisted that the US should unilaterally renounce its nuclear status before any new Authority was created. On 31 December 1946 the Soviet Union and Poland vetoed the Baruch Plan at a meeting of the Security Council. The Soviet rejection increased suspicions of Moscow in the US and undermined those who wanted to adopt a more accommodating attitude to the Soviet Union (Yergin, 1980: 240–1). However, given the implications of the Plan for state sovereignty it must be questioned whether the US government could have persuaded Congress to ratify any agreement that could have emerged, even if the USSR had been more sympathetic to Baruch's ideas.

As a result of these disagreements the Atomic Energy Commission lapsed into obscurity until the mid-1950s, though UN efforts to control nuclear weapons did continue. In fact some of the key Cold War agreements about nuclear weapons were agreed under the auspices of the UN. These include the 1963 Partial Test Ban Treaty and the 1968 Nuclear Non-Proliferation Treaty (Rogers, 1994).

Membership

The Cold War also affected the entry of new members into the UN because each superpower opposed applications from states in the other's bloc. The issue first arose in 1946 when Afghanistan, Albania, Iceland, Ireland, Jordan, Mongolia, Portugal and Sweden applied to the Security Council for membership. The US opposed the applications of Albania and Mongolia. The USSR objected to the admission of Ireland, Portugal and Jordan. None of these three applicants had diplomatic relations with Moscow. When the US proposed that all of these states should be accepted the USSR objected and insisted that each application be considered on its own merits. As a result the applications of Albania, Ireland, Mongolia, Jordan and Portugal were rejected, though Afghanistan, Iceland and Sweden were admitted. By 1953 there were 21 applications still pending (Lie, 1954: 101), and only six states had been able to obtain Security Council support and were admitted to the organization. They were Burma, Indonesia, Israel, Pakistan, Thailand and Yemen. The US had vetoed Bulgaria, Hungary, Rumania and Albania. The USSR had prevented Ireland, Jordan, Portugal, Italy, Austria, Japan and Ceylon joining the organization.

The Soviet Union very quickly had second thoughts about its opposition to 'package deals' whereby states allied to both blocs could be granted membership together. But now western states were opposed to this idea, and the US rejected several package-deal offers after 1946. In response a large number of vetoes were used by Moscow to keep pro-western states out. Indeed of the first 100 vetoes used at the UN, 51 were used to veto applications for membership (Boyd, 1971: 96–7). This issue was only resolved on 14 December 1955, when a package deal was constructed that obtained the support of both super-powers and was accepted by the General Assembly after it had been recommended by the Security Council. As a result 16 states became members of the UN: Albania, Austria, Bulgaria, Cambodia, Ceylon, Finland, Hungary, Ireland, Italy, Jordan, Laos, Libya, Nepal, Portugal, Romania and Spain. Japan was finally allowed to become a member in 1956, after the Soviet Union withdrew its veto. It adopted a foreign policy that gave an important place to 'UN-centrism'. In the next 20 years UN membership almost tripled. As we shall see, this resulted in the loss of a pro-western majority in the General Assembly. Morgenthau (1967: 469) has noted that with this increase in membership, 1955–6 'constitutes a turning point in the history of the United Nations, closing one phase and ushering in another'.

Korea

At the end of the Second World War Korea was divided into two territories along the 38th parallel of latitude. Two separate administrations emerged. North Korea came under the control of the USSR, South Korea was placed under American occupation. It was not surprising therefore, that at independence North Korea acquired a communist government and allied itself to Moscow whilst South Korea, under the author-itarian rule of President Syngman Rhee, aligned itself to Washington. Both governments regarded the division of their country as temporary and, as in Germany, partition created a conflict that was central to the Cold War.

As early as 14 November 1947 the General Assembly had established a nine-state Temporary Commission on Korea to examine the question of Korean independence. The Soviet

Union regarded this Commission as a US creation designed to deprive Moscow of an opportunity to use its right of veto on the Security Council. Therefore it refused to co-operate with it. So the Commission could only monitor the elections held in South Korea on 10 May 1948. North Korea also held elections, but without UN involvement. After South Korea obtained its independence the US and China (Formosa) attempted to obtain a Security Council Resolution to allow it to become a member of the UN, but this was vetoed by Moscow.

On 25 June 1950, after a series of clashes across the partition line, North Korea launched a military invasion of South Korea. This seemed to many to be a blatant act of aggression requiring a response from the UN. The UN's own Commission in Korea recommended mediation by a neutral mediator. The US, however, was anxious that a stronger response should be forthcoming from the UN.

When the Security Council met to discuss this matter the Soviet delegation was absent because Moscow was protesting about the refusal of the UN to give the Chinese seat to the new communist government in Beijing. Instead of recognising mainland China the Organization continued to recognise the old nationalist government of China, now based in Taiwan. The Soviet Union objected to this, and it began a policy of developing much closer relations with mainland China, a new communist power. On 14 February 1950 this Sino–Soviet alliance was cemented by the Treaty of Alliance, Friendship and Mutual Assistance.

The Soviet absence allowed the Security Council to pass three resolutions which legitimized US intervention in Korea under UN authority, though it is probable that the US would have taken military action even if the UN had not adopted these resolutions. The first declared that the North Korean invasion was a breach of the peace and called for the withdrawal of North Korean forces from South Korea. The second resolution recommended that member states assist South Korea. Forty-five states did provide some form of assistance, though many provided medical teams rather than military units. Sixteen states (in addition to South Korea) contributed military contingents for the UN-sponsored operation. These included the UK, France, Turkey, Australia and Canada. Most of the troop-contributing states were close allies of the US. However, the vast majority of ground, air and naval contingents came from the US and South Korea. The US provided half of the ground troops, 86 per cent of the naval forces and 93 per cent of the air forces (Whittaker, 1995: 42). The third Security Council resolution authorized a unified command using the UN flag, but under a commander desig-nated by the US. President Truman appointed General Douglas MacArthur as the Commanding General. When fundamental disagreements about the conduct of the war arose between Truman and MacArthur it was the US President, not the UN Secretary-General, who replaced the Commander.

Bowett (1957: 26–7) argues that these resolutions may not have been constitutional, since Article 27 of the Charter insists that 'the concurring votes of the permanent members' are needed to pass a substantive issue, and Article 28 states that when the Security Council meets each member shall be represented at all times. On these grounds the Soviet Union insisted that these resolutions on Korea were, therefore, illegal. Akehurst (1977: 196), on the other hand, argues that the actions of the USSR were in breach of their own obligations to the UN and claims that one interpretation of Article 28 of the Charter is that 'the absence of a permanent member ought not to prevent the Security Council from taking a decision'.

When the Soviet delegation returned, with its veto, the US was able to mobilize enough support to ensure that the organization could continue to play a role. To do this it persuaded the General Assembly to assert its authority by passing the 'Uniting for Peace' resolution (also called the 'Acheson Plan') on 3 November 1950. This allowed the General Assembly to take up an issue within 24 hours if the Security Council was prevented from exercising primary responsibility because of the use of the veto. In such cases the Assembly could make recommendations for collective measures. To assist its work a Peace Observation Commission was established, to observe and report in any area where a threat to international peace and security existed. A Collective Measures Committee was also created to co-ordinate actions by individual states. The 'Uniting for Peace' process could be invoked by a request from seven members of the Security Council or by a majority of the members of the UN.

However, the General Assembly, unlike the Security Council, does not have the ability to pass binding resolutions that states are obliged to act on. It can recommend or suggest a course of action; it cannot demand anything from states. Furthermore, the Assembly is larger and even more diverse than the Council, and so finds it harder to reach consensus on issues. For these reasons it is clear that the Assembly cannot provide a system of collective security with the certainty it needs if states are to put their trust in it. Bailey (1969: 3) notes that the General Assembly can be 'clumsy and unpredictable in a crisis'. Therefore, Claude (1984: 269) suggests, it may be better to regard the Uniting for Peace procedure as a device for collective legitimation rather than collective security: a mechanism whereby the US in particular obtained the moral support of the majority of UN members when the Soviet Union frustrated action by the Security Council.

The Washington-led operation in Korea very quickly drove the North Koreans back to the former partition line. However, in a fateful decision, the UN General Assembly then authorized General MacArthur to reunite the country by marching into North Korea. Despite warnings from the new communist government in Beijing the UN forces continued to advance up to the Yalu River, the border between North Korea and China. At this point the Chinese entered the conflict in massive numbers on the side of North Korea and pushed the UN troops back over the partition line. The General Assembly branded the People's Republic of China as aggressor and recommended an embargo against both it and North Korea. However, as the Soviet Union continued to support its communist allies, this embargo was never likely to be very effective.

After three years of bitter and costly fighting an armistice was signed in July 1953 at Panmunjon. One consequence of the war was that it became even more unlikely that communist China would replace nationalist China at the UN. The US position on this issue, fuelled by McCarthyism, hardened. The British government had recognized the communist government in China but was now unwilling to support its claim for a UN seat, whilst the French, already angered by Chinese support for Ho Chi Minh's independence struggle in Vietnam, now had another reason for a hostile attitude to Beijing. Even the Secretary-General, who was a supporter of communist Chinese membership, had to accept that this was not a position he could promote immediately after the war. Nonetheless, he continued to regret that over 400 million people were excluded from representation at the UN (Lie, 1954: Ch. XV).

Lie also paid a high price for his unavoidable support of UN action in Korea. Since the Soviet position was that many of the UN resolutions on the Korean War were illegal, they also argued that the Secretary-General had acted illegally in executing these decisions. Therefore, when Lie's term of office expired in February 1951 his re-nomination was vetoed by Moscow. As we shall see in the next chapter, Lie was able to carry on in office for another three years because he had the support of the General Assembly, but without Soviet backing and facing growing hostility in the US, he was eventually forced to resign.

Although many think of the Korean case as the only successful example of UN military action under Chapter VII during the Cold War, Morgenthau (1967: 297) is right to point out that the Korean incident 'made most members of the United Nations aware of the impotence of the Security Council . . . to discharge its functions as an agent of collective security'. Once the Soviet delegation returned to the UN, the Security Council was once again paralyzed by the veto.

Furthermore, it was clear that the Korean action was only made possible through US resolve and US resources. The action in Korea may have been 'collective' in the sense that it involved many states, but it was completely dependent on the US.

Veto and the hidden veto

We have seen in Chapter 1 how the 'Big Four' all supported the inclusion of the right of veto for permanent members of the Security Council and that without the veto it was unlikely that the great powers would have joined the UN. Certainly, all permanent members have used the veto but in the first 25 years the Soviet Union resorted to it the most. Between 1946 and 1955 there were 77 Soviet vetoes. The other three vetoes came from France (twice) and China. The Soviet vetoes were used to protect not just the interests of the USSR itself, but also to support states in its sphere of influence and to win the gratitude of certain other governments.

In Part II, paragraph two of the San Francisco Statement by the sponsoring powers, the 'Big Four' insisted that any disagreement on the Security Council about whether an issue was a substantive (vetoable) matter or a procedural (non-vetoable) matter would be considered a substantive issue. This gave the Soviet Union a legitimate basis for extending its power of veto, thereby deepening the paralysis of the Security Council. Thus when a vote was cast on certain issues at the Council and obtained the required majority, but the delegate from the USSR used a veto, the Soviets would argue that this matter was defeated. Other states might then argue that this was a procedural rather than a substantive matter, and so the veto could not be used. However, the USSR could then insist that the question of whether this was a procedural or sub-stantive issue should itself be put to the vote. According to the San Francisco Statement, this had to be treated as a non-procedural vote, where the USSR could use its veto to block any attempt to insist that the main resolution was only procedural. Then, the USSR, having overcome the claim that this was a purely procedural matter, could veto the main resolution (see Nicholas, 1959: 23–4).

Although the US did not use its power of veto until 1970, when it opposed a resolution that would have urged member states to sever relations with the minority white regime in Rhodesia, this was because Washington could exploit what has been called the 'hidden veto'. This could take two forms. First, the US could effectively stop a Security Council discussion by just threatening to use the veto. This would sometimes stop calls for the Security Council to meet because no productive outcome could be envisaged. Secondly, at least until the enlargement of the Council in 1965, the US could usually rely on the support of enough members of the Security Council (only three others were needed) to prevent the passage of unwelcome measures by denying them the required majority. After the influx of more third world states as non-permanent members in 1965 it became harder to outvote controversial proposals in this manner (Bailey, 1969: 74). It was now necessary to get six states to vote against a substantive proposal to stop it obtaining the required majority. Therefore from 1970 onwards we see Washington resorting to the veto on several occasions. Indeed, from this date it used the veto more frequently than the USSR. Whereas from 1945 to 1966 the USSR used its veto 75 times and the US did not veto once, between 1966 and 1993 the Soviet/Russian veto was used on 14 occasions, but the US used theirs 69 times (Roberts and Kingsbury, 1994: 19).

Claude (1984: 157–8) makes an important point about the veto when he argues that the real cause of the paralysis of the Security Council was the Cold War. The use of the veto was merely a symptom of this. It follows from this that the veto could, therefore, be regarded as a safety device, which warned the supporters of a measure not to push too hard against the state vetoing it; if they did they risked wider conflict. So, as Claude points out, some of the gravest crises for the UN occurred not as a result of the Soviet use of the veto but because the Soviet Union failed to use it on crucial issues – such as Korea or the Congo crisis of 1960. To protect their interest they then came into much greater conflict with the United Nations Organization.

The veto is also an important safety valve in another sense, for the ability of any one of the permanent members to stop action by the Security Council if it disagrees with a particular proposal means that the views of that member have to be taken into account in developing proposals. The veto may, therefore, encourage discussions between permanent members of the Security Council in order to devise measures that are acceptable to all five of them. In this sense the ever-present threat of the veto may be a catalyst for dialogue and compromise. Bailey (1969: 101) has shown that 'vetoes can be kept to a minimum if there is adequate diplomatic consultation *before* a proposal is presented and pressed to a vote' (emphasis in original).

In his thorough and comprehensive analysis Bailey has also noted that the use of the veto was rarely decisive in stopping the UN discussing an issue, or even taking action to uphold international peace and security. Claude (1984: 152) makes a similar point when he argues that from one perspective the UN's history can be described as 'a struggle by the United States to deprive the Soviet Union of its veto power, and by the latter to retain that power'. He believes that the United States has been more successful in this struggle.

Although the veto could delay UN action, a series of mechanisms were devised to by-pass deadlock on the Security Council. The most important one, as already noted, was the 'Uniting for Peace' resolution. This stated that

if the Security Council, because of lack of unanimity of the permanent members, fails to exercise its primary responsibility for the maintenance of international peace and security in any case where there appears to be a threat to peace, breach of the peace, or act of aggression, the General

Assembly shall consider the matter immediately with a view to making appropriate recommendations to members for collective measures.

Before this had been passed the US had also tried to divert decision-making to the General Assembly through the 'Little Assembly' idea. This resulted from an initiative by US Secretary of State George Marshall, who was frustrated by the inability of the Council to take action during the Greek Civil War because of the Soviet veto. So the US, western Europe and their allies used the General Assembly to adopt a resolution which created an Interim Committee, which could be summoned at short notice to discuss any matter referred to it by the Assembly. In fact, as Nicholas (1959: 49) notes, the Interim Committee 'was more significant as a symbol of frustration than as an escape from an impasse'. It never became an effective organ of the UN and has not been used since 1955.

Another device also allowed states to move an issue from the Council to the Assembly. Here the General Assembly was used to create special Commissions or to hold special sessions to consider specific cases. So in 1947 the General Assembly, at the request of the UK, held a special session to consider the future of Palestine. We have already seen how, in the same year, a US initiative led to the creation of an Interim Committee to consider the future of Korea. Other *ad hoc* commissions will be referred to in the next chapter.

Conclusion

Claude (1984: 261) is surely correct to argue that it is 'obvious that at no time have all or even most of the basic preconditions of collective security been realized, and that collective security has not become the operative system of international relations'. There are some who believe that collective security is an inherently flawed concept that can never be successfully applied in international relations. Claude takes this view, though he also seems to believe that it can contribute to an awareness of global responsibilities. Eban (1983: 264), a former Israeli foreign minister, agrees with this analysis and states:

> My conclusion is that collective security failed to take root as the central principle of international life, not because its adherents were unworthy of its vision or because its opponents were of small mind and ignoble disposition, but, more simply because it is not a very rational idea. It came on the scene in a world of nation-states and called upon states suddenly to behave in a way states have never behaved in the whole of history.

This is not the place to engage in this theoretical debate. Instead we shall merely point out that even if collective security is a viable concept, the international context within which the UN had to operate after 1945 was not supportive of a strong UN role and made it impossible to translate Chapter VII of the Charter into an effective mechanism to uphold international peace and security. Hoffmann (1968) has noted that the international system at this time was a 'revolutionary' one, where the superpowers represented very diverse political systems, and were in conflict not just because of geo-strategic considerations but because of major ideological differences about principles of justice and social organization. The system at the time was 'both bipolar – only two states have this capacity of "assured mutual destruction" – and furiously heterogeneous' (Hoffmann, 1987: 103). So even though the UN provided a common grammar, it lacked a 'community of values', and 'behind the common grammar there are competing ideological logics' (Hoffmann, 1981: 20).

Halliday (1994: 170) has taken up this theme, arguing that the Cold War should be characterized as an inter-systemic conflict 'in the sense that it is between two societies, or groups of societies, based on radically different, and incompatible, forms of social and political organization.' Furthermore, this confrontation was global in scope, and any conflict in the world could be, and often was, incorporated into the Cold War framework. In such a 'revolutionary' or 'inter-systemic conflict' constellation it was unlikely that the consensus required for an effective collective security system would be forthcoming.

Any restraint shown by the superpowers tended to be self-restraint, induced by the existence of nuclear weapons and the fear of mutual assured destruction. From this perspective the most momentous contribution to postwar peace between the great powers was the entry into the nuclear age, which took place between the opening of the San Francisco Conference and the entry into force of the Charter as a legally binding document. Furthermore, when the bonds of self-restraint slackened the UN could do nothing to affect the behaviour of either Washington or Moscow. Indeed the UN often became just another Cold War battleground. So, as Morgenthau (1967: 296) notes,

> The most important task of any such system [of law enforcement] is the imposition of effective restraints upon the struggle for power. This task the United Nations is incapable of performing at all where the need for its performance is greatest; that is, with respect to the great powers.

It was inevitable that the effectiveness and the credibility of the organization would, therefore, decline, since the paralysis of the Security Council meant that it was used less and less. Whereas between 1946 and 1948 it met on an average 132 times a year, in the 1950s it never met more than 72 times a year, and in 1959 only five meetings were held (Nicholas, 1959: 86). Even the technical, specialized agencies suffered from this Cold War competition. The USSR refused to join many of these agencies and withdrew from others. The Soviet client states also adopted an unco-operative attitude. Czechoslovakia, for example, left the FAO in 1948 and UNESCO and the IMF in 1949.

Nonetheless, the UN was not paralyzed completely, and did find useful roles for itself. Paradoxically, the heightened tensions and fears of the Cold War system that had eroded its collective security function probably made it more likely that states, when they could, would use it as a mechanism for conflict management and dispute settlement in order to avoid destructive superpower conflict. Increasingly, it was the General Assembly and the Secretariat which filled the gap left by the inability of the Council to respond constructively to threats to international peace and security in places like Korea, the Middle East and Africa.

3

FINDING A ROLE: THE UN, 1945–1981

> The Security Council . . . grappled only indirectly with the Cold War, the competition between American-led capitalism and Soviet-led communism. The Council's agenda was instead dominated by conflicts and crises arising out of decolonization. (Parsons, 1995: vii)

After 1945 the US- and Soviet-led blocs placed little credence in Chapter VII of the UN Charter. Instead they created two formidable military alliances, NATO and the Warsaw Treaty Organization, to guarantee their own interests. With an effective UN mechanism paralyzed even the smaller, non-committed states had to look elsewhere for a security policy. In Africa and Asia this eventually led to the creation of the Non-Aligned Movement at the start of the 1960s.

This failure of collective security during the Cold War and the exclusion of the UN from the main arenas of superpower confrontation could have led to a gradual erosion of the organization until it became superfluous to the workings of international politics. In fact, although the work of the UN was severely restricted by Cold War facts of life, it escaped the fate of the League of Nations and it was able to make some contributions to international peace and security between 1945 and 1981. The four Secretaries-General who led the UN during this period were able to find roles for themselves and this chapter will present an account of each Secretary-General's record in office.

The ability of the UN to play a role in upholding international peace and security after 1945 was due to a number of factors. Firstly, although the contest between the two superpowers was global in nature, not all conflicts in the world were seen as vital to the superpowers, even if these conflicts were always 'viewed through cold-war eyes' (Luard, 1982: 93). In fact, there were some conflicts that both Moscow and Washington had a mutual interest in managing because of the danger that escalation would lead to a major war between them, and perhaps even to their mutual annihilation. In such cases the UN proved a useful instrument of crisis management. Therefore, sometimes we see the US and the USSR working together at the UN to control potentially dangerous conflicts outside their own spheres of influence. For most of the Cold War era the region in this category that required most attention was, of course, the Middle East. There were four Arab–Israeli wars during the Cold War, in 1948–9, 1956, 1967 and 1973. There were also the Israeli invasions of Lebanon in 1978 and 1982. In all of these conflicts, as we shall see, the UN played some role.

A second reason why the UN was able to act to promote international peace and security is that Chapter VII is only one section of the Charter dealing with these issues. There is also Chapter VI. This deals with the pacific settlement of disputes and it enables the Security Council to 'investigate any dispute, or any situation which might lead to international friction' to determine if there is a threat to international peace and security (Article 34). It also entitles any member state to bring such a dispute to the attention of the Council or the Assembly (Article 35) and grants the Council the authority to 'recommend appropriate procedures or methods of adjustment'(Article 37). Many UN initiatives, including the majority of peacekeeping operations, drew their legitimacy from this chapter of the Charter.

Thirdly, as we have already seen, although the Security Council was unable to make a positive contribution in many Cold War conflicts because of the veto, it was possible to shift the centre of gravity of the organization away from it and towards the General Assembly through the 'Uniting for Peace' process, which was invoked several times in the 1950s to address peace and security matters. This was part of a definite move at the UN away from the paralyzed Security Council to the veto-free Assembly.

A final factor was that the Secretaries-General were able to use a broad definition of Article 99 of the Charter to play an activist role in peace and security matters. They were able to engage in quiet diplomacy and to work with the General Assembly and Security Council to establish peacekeeping forces. The four Secretaries-General who led the Organization during this period were, therefore, able to find roles for themselves and their organization. This may not be too surprising, for as Claude (1984: 7) has noted, the UN has no fixed purposes and develops through its political processes which are influenced by the aims of member states and the general state of the international system.

Trygve Lie (1946–1953)

Trygve Halvdan Lie had been the foreign minister of the Norwegian government-in-exile during the Second World War and had led the Norwegian delegation to the San Francisco Conference. In January 1946 he was nominated for the post of President of the General Assembly, but was defeated by the Belgian Paul-Henri Spaak, who had the support of the western states. However, shortly afterwards he emerged as a compromise candidate for the post of Secretary-General after the preferred choices of both the western states (van Kleffens of Holland or Lester Pearson of Canada) and the communist states (Simic of Yugoslavia) proved to be unacceptable. As a result Lie was elected by 46 votes to 3, and with the support of all the great powers.

Lie's most pressing task was to build up the Secretariat. Although a Preparatory Commission had already established its general structure and provisional staff regulations, new recruits with a wide range of skills had to be found and the role of the Secretariat had to be defined through practice. Whilst grappling with these matters and attempting to steer the UN through the storms of the Cold War the Secretariat also had to respond to emerging international crises.

Lie (1954: 158) noted in his autobiography that the Palestine issue was 'one of the most dramatic chapters of early United Nations history'. This was one of those conflicts that existed outside the superpowers' main areas of interest and, since Palestine was a League mandate administered by the UK, there was a history of international involvement and responsibility. After the Second World War the British were caught between the competing expectations of Jews and Arabs. On 2 April 1947 London requested the Secretary-General to put the Palestine issue on the General Assembly's agenda and to ask it, under Article 10 of the Charter, to make recommendations concerning the future of this territory. In response the Assembly met in special session and created the United Nations Special Committee on Palestine (UNSCOP), composed of representatives from Australia, Canada, Czechoslovakia, Guatemala, India, Iran, Netherlands, Peru, Sweden, Uruguay and Yugoslavia. It proposed that the British mandate should be terminated at the earliest practicable date and after a transition period under UN auspices, should be granted full independence. A majority of seven on UNSCOP proposed that Palestine be divided into Arab and Jewish states with Jerusalem retaining a special status as a UN trusteeship. A minority of three suggested that Palestine become a federal state.

On 29 November 1947 the General Assembly approved the majority plan by a vote of 33–13–10. Most of the 13 votes against came from Moslem countries, who opposed the creation of a separate Israeli state. Indeed, Arab states walked out of the Assembly after the vote and when the UN created a Palestine Commission to plan the transfer of rule from Britain to the three new entities the Arab states refused to co-operate with it. One of the ten abstainers was the UK, which took the rather unhelpful position that although they accepted the UN proposal, they would make no attempt to implement it. On 15 May 1948 the British threw the whole UN plan into turmoil when they made a sudden and complete withdrawal from Palestine. The first Arab–Israeli war began immediately when Egypt and Transjordan entered Palestine to protect the Arab population and to maintain 'security and order'.

As the situation in Palestine deteriorated the Secretary-General tried to establish an international force to keep the peace, but received no support from the Security Council. On 15 May Lie sent a letter to the permanent members pointing out that a failure to react would result in the 'most serious injury to the prestige of the United Nations' (Lie, 1954: 179). Yet no action was taken on this matter, though the Security Council did approve a suggestion by Lie that Count Bernadotte should be appointed as a UN mediator for Palestine. At his disposal was a Truce Commission of about 500 men, who stationed themselves along the Arab–Israeli cease-fire lines.

In June the UN became more active. A Security Council proposal for a four-week truce came into effect on 19 June, though Bernadotte was unable to make much progress in talks and the Arab governments resumed fighting on 9 July. The end of the truce prompted the Security Council to issue a strong resolution threatening sanctions against any party not complying with a new cease-fire. Bernadotte continued with his mediation attempts until he was murdered, with the French UN observer Colonel Serot, by Jewish terrorists on 17 September 1948. Ralph Bunch, Director of the UN's

Department for Trusteeship and Information from Non Self-Governing Territories, was appointed acting mediator and, on 24 February 1949, was able to produce an Israeli–Egyptian Armistice Agreement after 42 days of mediation on the island of Rhodes. Other agreements were then signed between Israel and Lebanon (1 March), Israel and Jordan (3 April), and Israel and Syria (20 July).

By signing the Armistice Agreement Tel Aviv and Cairo accepted the Security Council call for a cease-fire and Egyptian forces were withdrawn from the Al Faluja area. Israel was allowed to retain the Negev desert and an armistice commission was set up, under the UN Truce Supervision Organization (UNTSO) leadership, to supervise implementation of the terms of the Armistice. Bunch was awarded the Nobel Peace Prize for his work.

In May 1947, before the Palestine crisis, Lie (1954: 186) concluded that the 'spectacle in the Security Council so far has been a sad one'. However, at the start of 1949 he was willing to applaud the 'solid work' undertaken to bring peace to Palestine (Lie, 1954: 194). One of the main lessons Lie learned from the first Arab–Israeli conflict was that the UN needed to have an international force at its disposal, but Soviet opposition ensured that preliminary soundings on this matter were not allowed to make progress.

In Kashmir, as in Palestine, the UN became involved in another problem arising from partition. The majority of the population living in this disputed territory were Moslems, but the ruler (the Maharajah) was a Hindu. When the Indian subcontinent obtained its independence from Britain he refused to hold a plebiscite and, after an invasion of Kashmir by Pathan tribesmen from Pakistan, acceded to India. With tensions in the region high the matter was referred to the Security Council, which established a UN Commission for India and Pakistan (UNCIP). It was to investigate the situation in Kashmir and to offer its good offices and mediation to the parties. A UN Military Observer Group in India and

Pakistan (UNMOGIP) was also set up to observe the withdrawal of forces.

The UN also played a role in the Indonesian archipelago. At the end of the war British forces had landed in Java a month after Indonesian leaders had declared the country an independent state. Clashes with the British forces followed and the Dutch, the pre-war colonial power, continued to press for the reintroduction of their rule. In January 1946 the Ukraine made a complaint at the Security Council, arguing that the UN should support Indonesian independence, but the Dutch claimed that this was a domestic matter and that the UN had no right to interfere. Attempts by the Soviet bloc to set up a committee to investigate British actions were defeated, since western states supported Holland. Many of the European states were, of course, anxious that their own colonial possessions should not be threatened by claims of self-determination.

After talks between the parties broke down a 'police action' was conducted by the Dutch to retake their colony. In response the Security Council established a good-offices committee (composed of Belgium, Australia and the US) and a Consular Commission to report on whether a cease-fire agreement that had been agreed between the sides was being implemented. The work of the good-offices committee led to the Renville Agreement, named after the US warship on which the negotiations took place. This would have created an independent state – the United States of Indonesia – but one joined in a union with the Netherlands under the Dutch monarch. However, within a year Java, Sumatra and Madura would be allowed to hold a plebiscite to determine whether they wanted to remain part of this republic. Attempts to work out the details of this agreement proved difficult, and a more assertive position adopted at the Hague led to the collapse of the talks.

The Dutch then resorted to another 'police action', which alienated many states that had supported them up to this point. Most crucially, the US now turned against Holland and tabled a resolution at the Security Council calling for the withdrawal of forces and an investigation into who was responsible for the resumption of violence. This was too strong for Britain and France but did not meet the demands of the Soviet Union that the Dutch be labelled aggressors. Eventually a resolution was agreed which called for a cease-fire and the release of Indonesian leaders. Another resolution then called on the good-offices committee to make an urgent report on the situation in Indonesia. In the face of continuing Dutch 'intransigence' the Security Council then passed a remarkable resolution which set out a timetable for the implementation of Indonesian independence. The date set was 1 July 1950.

The Dutch, realizing that they were winning the military battles but losing the political war, now became more open to UN-sponsored talks. These led to an agreement that a round table conference would be convened in the Hague to establish a United States of Indonesia. The UN Consular Commission was one of the parties at the conference and helped to mediate some of the more difficult issues. Not all of these issues were settled, and the problem over the status of West New Guinea/West Irian continued to be a source of conflict between the Dutch and Indonesian governments. Nonetheless, progress was made and on 27 December 1949 Indonesia became an independent state. The UN had played a 'substantial role' in this process (Luard, 1982: 153), which had been relatively isolated from Cold War pressures.

However, conflicts that were central to the superpower confrontation provided less opportunity for effective UN involvement. In the case of Greece the UN created a Commission of Investigation which monitored this state's northern border to check claims that communist states were aiding the communist forces in the Greek Civil War. When the Commission reported that there was evidence that Yugoslavia, Albania and Bulgaria were providing such help, the USSR vetoed Security Council resolutions based on this report's recommendations. The western states then switched focus to the Assembly. Here the US introduced a proposal that had already been vetoed in the Council. It called on the UN to establish a permanent committee to monitor the border between Greece and its communist neighbours. This was passed by a large majority, and the UN Special Committee in the Balkans (UNSCOB) was set up. Communist states, however, refused to serve on it. UNSCOB produced a series of reports on the Greek civil war, which confirmed that Yugoslavia, Albania and Bulgaria continued to support the communist guerrillas, who also used the territory of these states for sanctuary. UNSCOB also confirmed that the communist guerrillas had moved large numbers of Greek children into Bulgaria. The USSR claimed that they were refugees, but the US argued that they were being trained and indoctrinated to continue the fight on the communist side.

UNSCOB was wound up by the Assembly in 1951, by which time the civil war had ended and cross-border support for the guerrilla movement had declined to a much smaller level. Luard (1982: 131) concludes that the UNSCOB case 'showed the difficulty the organization had in this period in dealing with cold-war issues'. He also regrets that the UN, led by its pro-US majority, handled this issue in a partisan way and did nothing to promote negotiations between the main adversaries.

During the Czechoslovakian crisis of 1948 Stalin finally destroyed the remaining democratic elements in that country. The UN was unable to offer any effective assistance to the Czech people even though the UN representative of the over-thrown government, Jan Papanek, called on the Organization to investigate what had happened in his country. Some western states proposed establishing a sub-committee to examine the issue. But under the threat of a Soviet veto the issue was never pursued with much enthusiasm and this limp proposal came to nothing.

During the Berlin crisis of 1948–9 the Security Council did consider the blockade imposed by Stalin on those zones of Berlin under the control of western states. But Moscow refused to play any part in the discussions and vetoed any attempt to pass resolutions that were in any way critical of its actions. So all the Security Council could do was to refer the issue to a committee of experts. Lie was also able to use American and Soviet UN staff members to open up channels of communication with Moscow and Washington and the UN was involved in attempts to draw up a plan for currency reform in Germany, which had been the issue that had triggered Stalin's blockade. However, these discussions led nowhere and eventually Stalin was forced to end the blockade when the western states organized a successful airlift to circumvent the obstacles to free movement into West Berlin on the ground. The two sides did meet at the UN to determine the exact terms of an agreement on Berlin, by which all restrictions were to be removed on 12 May 1949.

Goodwin (1957: 239–40) claims that there were two main lessons that were drawn from the UN's role in this crisis. The first was that the relative failure of mediation showed that on matters of vital interest 'solutions advocated by supposedly disinterested third . . . parties were likely to fall on deaf ears'. The second was that the 'Council's main value was as a point of diplomatic contact, particularly but not only between the Soviet Union and the West'.

We have seen in the last chapter how Lie had upset the USSR because of the strong anti-Communist approach they believe he had taken during the Korean War and because Moscow regarded his actions as 'illegal' because they were based on UN resolutions which were deemed to be unconstitutional. In 1949 Lie had been informed by the USSR that they wished him to serve a second term as Secretary-General. However it came as no surprise when, just a year later, the Soviet delegation vetoed his re-appointment and Lie was able to remain in office only because the US threatened to veto any other candidate. In these circumstances a deadlock was only avoided when the General Assembly voted by a large majority (46-5-8) to allow him to 'continue in office' for three years from 1 February 1951. However Lie had to face growing

Soviet opposition, and he was boycotted by Moscow in both an official and personal capacity.

It is difficult to judge whether this pressure contributed to what some see as a lack of judgement in what was one of the most controversial decisions made by Lie as Secretary-General. By 1952 the anti-Communist hysteria in the US was at its height and the McCarthy witch-hunts began focusing on US citizens working in the UN Secretariat. In late 1952 a US federal grand jury claimed that it had uncovered evidence that US communists had 'infiltrated' the UN in large numbers. Shortly after, 18 US citizens employed by the Organization were called to hearings of the Internal Security Subcommittee of the Senate Judiciary Committee. Here, on legal advice, they refused to testify and invoked the Fifth Amendment of the US Constitution, which allows a person to decline to answer questions if this could result in self-incrimination.

Lie, facing a hostile public in the US, then suspended these employees and established a Commission of Jurists to give advice on disciplinary action that could be taken against them. It advised that a refusal to testify when challenged with claims of subversive activities was an act of serious misconduct and a breach of contract which forbids UN employees from engaging in activities incompatible with the proper discharge of duties. The Secretary-General was also advised that he could dismiss any employees on these grounds. All US citizens who had pleaded the Fifth Amendment were then sacked by Lie after being given an opportunity to give a satisfactory explanation of their refusal to testify. None of these were ever charged with any crime by the US government.

Those who were employed by the UN on permanent contracts then took their cases to a UN Administrative Tribunal, which disagreed with the Commission of Jurists' decision that refusal to testify by claiming a constitutional privilege was 'serious misconduct', and so concluded that their summary dismissal was unlawful. The International Court of Justice agreed with the Tribunal in an opinion given in July

1954. But instead of reinstating these sacked employees Lie decided to pay them compensation, though the US Congress decided that no US funds allocated to the UN were to be used for this purpose. In an even more controversial decision Lie then allowed the Federal Bureau of Investigation to set up an office within the UN Headquarters in New York to vet applications from US citizens.

Lie has been criticised by many for his actions in this case. The speed with which he gave into US demands had a deep, adverse impact on the morale of the Secretariat and did nothing to affect the hostile attitude to the UN that existed in many quarters in the US. If anything, it increased suspicion and distrust of the organization. Hazzard (1973), who worked at the UN Secretariat for ten years, was one of the strongest critics of Lie's actions. She claims that he drove able people out of the UN (the General Legal Counsel of the UN, Abraham Feller, even committed suicide when under investigation), compromised his own position with the USSR, and may even have violated Article 100 of the Charter, which states that 'in the performance of their duties the Secretary-General and the staff shall not seek or receive instructions from any government or from any other authority external to the organization'.

Trygve Lie played a significant role in shaping the Secretariat. As Boyd (1962: 90) points out, before he left Lie had won the following rights: to make major political proposals in public and private and to table resolutions; to establish missions of inquiry; to send envoys; to criticise member governments publicly; and to demand action from the Council. However, Lie's authority, credibility and effectiveness were eventually ground down as a result of Cold War tensions. His own 'Twenty-Year Programme for Peace', designed to improve the role of the UN during the Cold War, was stillborn. He learnt that although the Secretary-General was able to find some freedom of action, the limits were set by the great powers. But against the deep divisions of the Cold War how could any activist Secretary-General, working for the 'international interest', function at all without eventually upsetting either

Washington or Moscow? This was the dilemma facing Lie's successor.

Dag Hammarskjøld (1953–1961)

Lie announced his intention to resign on 10 November 1952, before the end of the extra three years he had been granted by the General Assembly. Some west-European states and the Commonwealth wanted Lester Pearson of Canada to replace Lie. The US supported General Romulo of the Philippines. Moscow backed the Polish Foreign Minister Skrzeszewski, but also proposed the Indian V. L. Pandit. As the permanent members of the Security Council could not agree on any of these names Dag Hammarskjøld of Sweden, first proposed by France, emerged as the compromise candidate. He became the new Secretary-General on 10 April 1953 when this decision was endorsed by the General Assembly. In September 1957 he was unanimously re-appointed for another five-year term.

Many of those who voted for him thought that he would be a discrete, quiet, 'safe', technocrat. It is said that the US Secretary of State, Dulles, had never heard of Hammarskjøld before his election (Boyd, 1962: 101). Yet, in his first speech after his re-appointment in 1957, he revealed himself as a more activist head of the UN. Here he stated that 'the Secretary-General should be expected to act also without such guidance, should this appear to him necessary in order to help in filling any vacuum that may appear in the systems which the Charter and traditional diplomacy provide for the safeguarding of peace and security' (Boyd, 1962: 103).

Hammarskjøld, another Scandinavian, was a youthful 47 when he accepted his new position at the UN. At that time he was a shy, serious and solitary minister in the Swedish Foreign Office. When he took over the leadership of the Secretariat the Cold War was entering one of its periodic thaws. This was caused by a number of factors that included the death of Stalin

63

and the end of the Korean War. In 1955 Khrushchev, who won the power struggle for control of the Kremlin, initiated a policy of 'peaceful coexistence' between East and West. He also placed more emphasis than Stalin on the UN as an instrument of Soviet foreign policy and upgraded the role of the Organization. During the Stalin years very little was published in the USSR about the UN (Dallin, 1962: 89). Now many indicators revealed a more positive attitude. For example, the UN started to receive a more favourable press and in 1956 the Soviet branch of the United Nations Association was established (Dallin, 1962: 39–40). The first full-length book about the role of the Soviet Union in the UN appeared in 1957 and other important works followed (Dallin, 1962: 90).

Hammarskjøld used this period of relative stability to make an impressive start to his leadership. In December 1954 he was mandated by the General Assembly to seek the release of 11 US fliers who had been captured during the Korean War when serving with the UN forces. After a period of quiet diplomacy, that did much to enhance his credibility, all these men were released in August 1955. However, the limitations of his position were revealed the same year when the US effectively blocked any discussion of their intervention in Guatemala to remove the reformist government of Arbenz. Washington insisted that this was a matter for the Organization of American States. Hammarskjøld argued that this did not preclude the UN from considering the matter, but the pro-US bloc on the Council was able to stop the inclusion of the issue on its agenda.

Hammarskjøld's first major test, however, occurred in 1956 in the Middle East, a region where the superpowers were now aligning themselves on opposite sides. After President Nasser of Egypt nationalized the Suez Canal Company Britain and France entered into a secret agreement with Israel whereby an Israeli invasion of Egypt would provide an excuse for these two states to launch a military attack on the Nasser regime, thereby removing a threat to Anglo–French interests in the Middle East. However, this ill-conceived operation quickly ran into trouble when the Eisenhower administration in the US opposed it. Moscow, engaged at the same time in a military intervention in Hungary, also made threats against London and Paris. Because of the use of the veto by the British and French representatives on the Security Council, the 'Uniting for Peace' procedure was invoked to allow the General Assembly to discuss this problem. From 1 November 1956 an emergency special session was convened which called for an immediate cease-fire, the withdrawal of forces and prompt action to re-open the Suez canal. The British and French agreed to do this provided that a UN force was deployed. Hammarskjøld was asked to develop a plan for the deployment of a United Nations Emergency Force, an idea proposed by Lester Pearson of Canada. Moscow abstained in the vote that established this force, but it did not vote against. The Suez crisis showed how the UN could undertake constructive action. It allowed the British and French forces to withdraw without too much loss of face, and helped to stabilize the border between Egypt and Israel.

Perhaps the most important outcome of the Suez crisis for the UN was this 'invention' of UN peacekeeping. Other multinational forces had been deployed in the past by the League of Nations, in Upper Silesia in 1921 and the Saar in 1935. The UN itself had created missions to the Middle East (UNTSO), the Balkans (UNSCOB) and Kashmir (UNMO-GIP). Indeed, by 1956 over one thousand men had already served with these operations (Boyd, 1962: 158). But these had been observer missions. UNEF was the 'real debut' of UN peacekeeping (Rikhye, 1984: 4).

After the General Assembly had given its authorization, the Secretariat created a force of about 6000 men from ten states (Brazil, Canada, Colombia, Denmark, Finland, India, Indonesia, Norway, Sweden and Yugoslavia) and the last British and French troops left before the end of December 1956. There is a famous saying by Hammarskjøld that peacekeeping is not a job for a soldier, but only a soldier can do it, and Walter Lippmann pointed out the originality and sublime feature of a concept that requires soldiers to promote peace rather than wage war (Liu, 1990: 3).

There is no official UN definition of peacekeeping. The most commonly accepted characterization is the one developed by the International Peace Academy in New York. It describes peacekeeping as:

> the prevention, containment, moderation and termination of hostilities between or within states through the medium of third-party intervention, organized and directed internationally, using multinational military, police and civilian personnel to restore and maintain peace. (see, for example, Rikhye, 1984: 1–2)

The crucial features that contributed to the success of UNEF and became the key principles that underpinned many future peacekeeping missions were produced at this time. First, the force depended on the consent of the parties to the conflict. This, in turn, required that the UN operate in an impartial manner and not attempt to implement a particular political settlement. This principle of neutrality is strongly stated by General Rikhye, an Indian soldier with considerable UN peacekeeping experience. He has written that in such peace-keeping enforcement plays no part and the 'fundamental principles are those of objectivity and non-alignment with the parties to the dispute, ideally to the extent of total impartiality from the controversial issues at stake' (Rikhye, 1983: 6).

Second, military force was to be used in a restrained fashion and only in self-defence and as a last resort. Any breach of this principle would threaten the UN's impartiality and would move it away from peacekeeping to peace-enforcement. This would be a major threat to a traditional peacekeeping mission that depended more on moral authority than on an unobtainable military superiority. Third, the force was to have the support of both superpowers. Fourth, it was composed of contingents from states with no vested interest in the conflict and units from the permanent members of the Security

Council were not included. This also protected the impartiality of the operation. Fifth, it worked on the basis of a realistic mandate.

The General Assembly decided that UNEF would be funded according to a formula whereby the great powers would pay proportionately more than the smaller states. The USSR consistently refused to pay its contribution, arguing that the force was illegal, since it had not been created by the Security Council. In the case of UNEF, and later in the Congo, it was the US that made up some of the deficit through voluntary contributions, though this itself raised serious questions about the independence of the Organization.

The inability of the Organization to do anything to stop or reverse the Soviet invasion of Hungary, which occurred at the same time as the British and French invasion of Suez, reminded the UN of the limits within which it had to work. Predictably, the USSR vetoed a US-sponsored Security Council resolution which would have called on Moscow to 'desist forthwith' from intervening in the internal affairs of Hungary and to withdraw their troops without delay. The Uniting for Peace procedure was then invoked and the General Assembly met in Emergency Special Session, but this had little impact on the situation in Eastern Europe. Hammarskjøld was mandated to investigate the Soviet invasion, but with no co-operation forthcoming from Moscow the UN could do little.

After his re-election in 1957 Hammarskjøld 'steadily developed the idea of an active role for the United Nations through practical demonstrations of what the Organization could do' (Urquhart, 1972: 255). From this time the Secretary-General adopted a technique of publicly presenting an 'interpretation' or 'assumption' about UN resolutions or the Charter. If this was not challenged he would later cite his interpretation as a precedent to be used in other situations (Boyd, 1962: 109).

The Middle East remained volatile, and the growing influence of Nasser in the region, combined with the overthrow of the pro-western Hashemite monarchy in Iraq, alarmed the US, who believed that it could result in a greater communist presence. In these circumstances the UN was able to assist with crisis management. For example, in Lebanon in 1958 the General Assembly requested that Hammarskjøld facilitate the withdrawal of foreign troops. To this end he strengthened the UN Observer Group in Lebanon (UNOGIL) that was already in place to investigate charges of foreign infiltration, and he played an important role in the General Assembly's emergency session on Lebanon.

A year after the Lebanon initiative Hammarskjøld also played a significant role in a dispute between Cambodia and Thailand over the Preah Vihear temple complex. On his own initiative he appointed Baron Johan Beck-Friis of Sweden as his special representative. Talks between the parties then led to the release of prisoners and the re-opening of the frontier between the two states. The case was eventually decided by the International Court of Justice. Hammarskjøld also used his good offices in a dispute between Tunisia and France that was related to the war in Algeria, and a dispute between the UK and Saudi Arabia over the Bureimi Oasis. He also tried unsuccessfully to help resolve the conflict over Laos but ran up against superpower interests in the region.

The biggest challenge for Hammarskjøld came in Africa. This followed an extensive tour of the continent which led him to believe that the UN should play a leading role in the 'proper development' of this continent (Urquhart, 1972: 382). The test came quickly, in June 1960, when the Belgian Congo obtained its independence and plunged straight into a civil war that included a secessionist movement in the mineral-rich province of Katanga and Belgian military intervention. After receiving a letter from the new government asking the UN to protect the state of the Congo from 'external aggression' Hammarskjøld used Article 99 to bring the conflict there to the attention of the Security Council. The Council authorized the dispatch of a peacekeeping force (ONUC) which at its peak was composed of 20 000 personnel. Most of these troops were from African states, but there were also contingents from India, Sweden and Ireland. The Council also called on

Belgium to withdraw its troops. ONUC was deployed to assist the government of the Congo in maintaining law and order but was not meant to enforce any specific political solution. Here the UN found itself enmeshed in a far more complicated situation than that faced by UNEF in the Sinai, and many of the factors that contributed to UNEF's success were absent in the Congo. The mandate was less realistic. The force's impartiality was lost when it adopted a vigorous anti-secessionist stance, and the superpowers then became divided in their attitude to the force.

At the start of the operation both the USA and the USSR could see a positive role for ONUC and both voted in favour of it in the Security Council. However, the government of the Congo disintegrated into competing groups and ONUC was then perceived by Moscow to be working for the interests of the west against the faction it supported. The Soviets, who were supporting Prime Minister Lumumba, complained about one incident in particular, when the UN representative, Andrew Cordier (an American), closed the airports and shut down the national radio. Cordier claimed this was to stop the outbreak of civil war, but Moscow believed that these actions fatally undermined the Lumumba faction. Hammarskjøld then became a prime target of Soviet attack when he carried on with the Congo operation with General Assembly authority after the USSR had vetoed the continuation of ONUC at the Security Council.

The Soviet Union retaliated by raising a radical proposal to alter the very nature of the office of the Secretary-General. They wanted the leadership of the Secretariat to pass to a three-man 'troika' (the three-horse Russian sledge), with each of the three members representing a different bloc of states: the west, the communist world and the non-aligned. The idea was proposed by the Soviet leader Khrushchev in a speech to the General Assembly in September 1960. Soviet spokesmen also suggested that the idea could be applied to other UN bodies.

In September 1961 Hammarskjøld decided that he had to travel to the region for talks with Tshombe, but was killed when his plane crashed near Ndola in Northern Rhodesia. A UN inquiry delivered an open verdict about the cause of the crash. After the death of Hammarskjøld, the troika plan, which had never obtained much support at the UN, was shelved. As Kyle (1995: 19) notes, it 'was a tribute to the standing of Dag Hammarskjøld that the Communist line found no answering echo'.

It was to Hammarskjøld's credit that he was able to develop the role of the Secretary-General in the manner that he did. He constantly sought a more active role for his organization and his term of office saw the development of peacekeeping as one of the UN's major tools for protecting international peace and security. His 'quiet diplomacy' also led to a significant increase in the 'presence' of the Organization in international politics. His most important biographer has noted that he 'was very skilful in taking full advantage of [the] political environment and in using it to foster and increase the UN's effectiveness' (Urquhart, 1972: 595).

U Thant (1961–1971)

After Hammarskjøld's tragic death, U Thant of Burma was appointed as Acting Secretary-General for the remaining portion of Hammarskjøld's term. In November 1962 he was then appointed for a five-year term, though this was deemed to have started when he took over from Hammarskjøld. This meant that he had to be re-appointed in 1966. After some uncertainty about whether U Thant wanted to stand again, he did eventually accept an appeal to continue in office and was re-appointed by a unanimous vote in both the Council and the Assembly.

The Burmese diplomat was a quiet, honourable man and a devout Buddhist. He had been the Permanent Representative of Burma at the UN since 1956. At a time when the Cold War rivalries were threatening to tear the UN apart his uncontroversial and skilful approach did much to save the 'prestige, independence and effectiveness of his office' (Skjelsbaek, 1991: 103).

U Thant inherited the complicated Congo problem. At the end of 1961 he took a tough line and ordered ONUC, which was being subjected to attacks from the secessionist forces led by Tshombe, to re-establish law and order in the Katangan capital of Elisabethville. This robust action caused considerable disquiet in western Europe, but it was an important contribution to the re-establishment of the authority of the central government.

ONUC was withdrawn in June 1964. However, before it was wound up it triggered a serious financial crisis at the UN, which arose because of the unwillingness of the USSR and France to pay their assessed contributions for the force. Moscow argued that it was not bound by this because it had not been approved by the Security Council. The US invoked Article 19 of the Charter which states that any member that does not pay its assessed contributions for over two years could lose voting rights in the Assembly. If applied against the USSR, a course of action supported by Washington, it was certain to spark a major constitutional crisis at the UN. In July 1962 the International Court of Justice at the Hague issued an Advisory Opinion (by nine votes to five) that these assessed contributions for both UNEF and ONUC were legally binding on states. Although this opinion was challenged by both the USSR and France, the General Assembly accepted it by an overwhelming majority.

The Secretary General was anxious to avoid a damaging confrontation, and with the help of some member states worked to avert a major showdown. When a new peacekeeping force was created for Cyprus in March 1964, it was decided that this would be funded by voluntary contributions only, though this has also proved to be an unsatisfactory option. The UN Temporary Executive Authority established for West New Guinea, created in 1963, was paid for by Holland and Indonesia. Yet still the issue threatened to erupt at the 1964 General Assembly, postponed until December to provide more time for a compromise to be worked out. However, no agreement could be found, and so U Thant proposed that the business of the General Assembly should proceed for that session with no vote being taken on any issue. This would side-step the issue of whether voting rights should be withdrawn. However, it meant that the Assembly could not debate any politically sensitive matter. The financial crisis then fizzled out in 1965, partly because the controversial ONUC deployment had ended in 1964 and partly because the US accepted that the majority of UN members did not support a tough line on Article 19.

The most serious direct superpower confrontation of the Cold War occurred in October 1962, when the US discovered that the USSR was building nuclear missile sites on the island of Cuba, 90 miles from US territory. The US insisted that this activity should cease, even though it had located missiles in Turkey, which bordered the Soviet Union. In support of this decision a naval blockade of dubious international legality was imposed on Cuba and naval commanders were instructed to stop Soviet ships on their way to the island. At the height of the crisis, when no-one was sure if a direct military confrontation could be avoided, U Thant wrote to both US President Kennedy and Soviet leader Khrushchev urging them to do everything possible to avoid confrontation, though it is unlikely that these letters played any significant role in determining the outcome of the crisis. U Thant also visited the Cuban leader, Fidel Castro, in Havana. This was a more important initiative because Castro was threatening to undermine a Soviet–US agreement whereby Moscow would withdraw its missiles under UN supervision in return for a US pledge to lift the blockade and not to invade the island. Castro, who had been kept on the sidelines by Moscow, insisted that Cuba receive further guarantees of its security before he would allow the plan to be implemented. During these talks Castro agreed to return the body of US pilot Rudolph Anderson, who had been killed on a surveillance mission over the island, but U Thant could not get Castro's permission for a UN presence in

Cuba. However, during this visit U Thant received assurances from the Soviet ambassador that the missile sites were being dismantled, which allowed the Secretary-General to claim that his mission had been a success. Talks between US and Soviet representatives at UN headquarters eventually led to an agreement whereby the US dropped its insistence on UN supervision of the missile withdrawal in return for an assurance that US reconnaissance flights over the island would not be fired on.

In other international crises the Secretary-General was able to play a more direct role. In 1962 the Dutch and Indonesian governments agreed, after UN mediation by Ellsworth Bunker, that West Irian should come under the control of Jakarta. As part of the transition process the territory would be ruled by a UN Temporary Executive Authority (UNTEA), which was to govern the territory between 1 October 1962 and 30 April 1963. In order to help preserve law and order during this period a UN Security Force (UNSF) was deployed. In this way a long-standing international problem was resolved. However, no attempt was made to obtain the consent of the people of West Irian before they were handed over to Indonesia. The 1962 agreement did require that a plebiscite be held in 1969 in West Irian to determine the future of the territory. By this time the Indonesian authorities had consolidated their control and although a plebiscite of sorts was held there remains a feeling that the people of West Irian were steamrollered into a union with Indonesia.

At the end of 1963, after three years of peaceful but fragile independence, intercommunal violence erupted between the Greek and Turkish communities in Cyprus. This presented a clear threat to international peace and security because of the real danger that Greece and Turkey would be drawn into war over the island. When a British plan to introduce a NATO force proved impractical the matter was taken to the Security Council, which in March 1964 created the United Nations Force in Cyprus (UNFICYP). At its peak the force was composed of just under 6500 personnel.

UNFICYP was the first UN operation to make effective use of civilian police contingents. The force did much good work and helped reduce levels of violence on the island, though it could not do this on all occasions. Nonetheless Hart (1990: 120) claims that UNFICYP 'proved vital to the maintenance of general peace'. Resolution 186 also asked the Secretary-General to appoint a mediator, and U Thant selected Sakari Tuomioja of Finland. Galo Plaza took over following Tuomioja's sudden death in August 1964. Plaza resigned in 1965 after his report on the Cyprus issue was rejected by Turkey because it retained the idea that Cyprus should remain a unified state.

In August 1965 the UN-observed cease-fire in Kashmir broke down when fighting erupted between India and Pakistan. U Thant attempted to restore the status quo by appealing to the parties and by flying to the region for talks with President Ayub Khan of Pakistan and Prime Minister Shastri of India. In November the Security Council called on the two governments to meet with a representative of the Secretary-General (Tulio Marambrio of Chile). However in this case the key mediator was Soviet Premier Kosygin, who was able to end hostilities at a meeting in Tashkent.

We have already noted that one of the key principles of what is now called traditional or 'first-generation' peacekeeping is that it depends on the consent of the host state. On 16 May 1967, as the Middle East was drifting towards a third Arab–Israeli war, President Nasser revealed this to be a weakness when he requested that UNEF should be immediately removed from Egyptian territory. This would allow the Egyptian army to take control of strategic positions at Sharm el Sheikh and El Sabha, and would be a demonstration of resolve to Syria, which had accused Nasser of hiding behind the UN. The UN believed that the withdrawal of UNEF would make war in the region more likely, yet U Thant informed the troop-contributing states that he would have no option but to comply with Nasser's request. He asked the Israeli government if it would accept a re-deployment of the force to the Israeli side of the border, but this was rejected. This did not stop Israeli representatives criticising the Secretary-General for his decision to remove the force.

U Thant also flew to Cairo for a meeting with Nasser, but was unable to change the mind of the President. The decision to remove UNEF attracted a lot of criticism at the time, and some believe that the rapid withdrawal of the force hastened the onset of war. U Thant's defence was that he had to respect the sovereign status of Egypt, but some commentators argued that the peacekeepers were removed too quickly, and more could have been done to delay their departure in order to try and stabilize the ongoing Middle East crisis. However, this seems to over-estimate the ability of the UN to prevent war, and ignores the possibility that several contingents would have withdrawn their units unilaterally if they judged that U Thant was exposing them to danger by delaying their departure.

The outbreak of the Six Day War on 5 June triggered extensive diplomatic activity in New York. The Security Council issued several ineffectual cease-fire calls, though on 10 June both Syria and Israel accepted one such plea. The decisive Israeli victory allowed it to extend the territory under its control and to 'reunite' Jerusalem. A Special Emergency Session of the General Assembly passed a resolution declaring 'null and void' any change in the status of Jerusalem, a Holy City to Jews and Moslems, but this was rejected by the euphoric Israeli side.

The most substantial UN contribution to the discussions about the Arab–Israeli conflict came in November 1967, when Security Resolution 242 was adopted. This became a cornerstone of most peace initiatives in the region from that time on. The key feature of the resolution was the 'land for peace' formula. By this the sovereignty and territorial integrity of Israel would be recognised by Arab states and Israel would withdraw from occupied territories seized in the 'recent conflict', though considerable disagreements would arise over whether Israel had to withdraw from *all* of these territories. Kissinger (1982: 197) once remarked that one problem with

Resolution 242 is that although it used fine-sounding words like 'lasting peace' and 'secure borders' it 'does not define the adjectives'. The Resolution also requested the Secretary-General to appoint a Special Representative to promote agreement. The Swedish diplomat Gunnar Jarring was given this difficult role but made very little progress in his 'mission impossible' to promote dialogue.

The ineffectiveness of the UN was also revealed during the invasion of Czechoslovakia by the Warsaw Pact states in August 1968. This was an attempt by the Kremlin to shore up hard-line communist rule, under threat from reformers. On the day of the invasion the US and Denmark requested a meeting of the Security Council. The next day it discussed a Danish draft resolution which declared Warsaw Pact actions to be a violation of the Charter and called on the Warsaw Pact forces to be withdrawn. Predictably, the USSR vetoed it when it came to a vote, claiming that there was no basis for a meeting of the Council because the Warsaw Pact states had been invited in at the request of the Czech government and that they were there to protect its people from counter-revolutionary forces. This claim prompted George Ball, the US Ambassador to the UN, to reply that the sort of fraternal assistance that the Soviets were showing the Czechs was the 'kind that Cain showed Abel' (Ball, 1982: 441).

The Soviet position was dramatically undermined when both the Czech foreign minister and the Presidium of the Czechoslovakian National Assembly criticised the military intervention. There were also numerous attacks on Soviet actions in that year's General Assembly. Boyd (1971: 315) rather generously argues that the UN was able to help 'to illuminate both the reality behind the Russians' veils of illusion and the extent to which world opinion had been outraged by the invasion'. This cannot hide the fact that the Organization failed to take decisive action, though Urquhart (1987: 221) is probably correct to argue that in such cases the UN becomes a focus for public indignation as western societies attempt to assuage their guilt.

The UN was also excluded from the sphere of influence of the other superpower. This was best illustrated by the events in the Dominican Republic in 1965. In April that year US troops invaded this state to stop a socialist government coming to power. Criticisms of the US action by the Soviet Union, France and several Latin American states had little impact, and calls for a greater UN role were ignored by the Johnson administration in Washington, which informed the UN that the Organization of American States (OAS) had been asked to consider the situation there. So it was the OAS that sent an international force to the Dominican Republic composed of 22 000 US troops and much smaller contingents from Brazil, Honduras, Nicaragua, Paraguay and Costa Rica. The only role that the UN played in this conflict was to dispatch a representative of the Secretary-General, Jose Antonio Mayobre of Venezuela, and a small group of military advisors to monitor the situation.

We have already noted how both US attitudes and the Korean War frustrated Lie's attempts to have the People's Republic of China admitted to membership of the UN. In fact it took nearly 20 years to bring this about. It was not until October 1971, as Cold War tensions eased and superpower *détente* blossomed, that the General Assembly voted by 75 to 35 (with 17 abstentions) to recognise the representatives of the People's Republic of China 'as the only legitimate representatives of China to the United Nations'. So in the last year of the U Thant Secretary-Generalship, Communist China (population one billion) replaced Taiwan (population sixteen million) as the legitimate representative of China. After taking its seat the Chinese government tended to support third world states on economic matters, but played a subdued role in security matters.

One feature of the U Thant years was the unwillingness of the UN to involve itself in what were thought of as internal wars in multi-ethnic post-colonial societies. In practice, of course, this policy of non-involvement usually favoured the status quo and the governments challenged by secessionist movements. U Thant's position was made clear during the costly war in Nigeria between 1966 and 1969. The Secretary-General took the view that the UN 'has never accepted and does not accept and I do not believe it will ever accept the principle of secession of a part of its member state' (Buchheit, 1978: 87). In the Bangladesh case U Thant was involved in a secret but ineffectual initiative to promote dialogue between the parties (U Thant, 1977: 424–5). However, on the whole, the 'involvement of the United Nations in the Bangla Desh crisis was limited and ineffective' (Buchheit, 1978: 209). The US did attempt to obtain a Security Council resolution criticising India's invasion of East Pakistan/Bangladesh, but it was vetoed by the Soviet Union. Washington then invoked the Uniting for Peace procedure to obtain a vote against India, but it had little impact on the situation.

Another significant failure occurred during the Vietnam War, a conflict which dominated US foreign policy for most of the 1960s. Washington was opposed to any UN involvement in this conflict, and for most of the war the matter was not even discussed by the Security Council. As early as August 1964 U Thant had proposed to Secretary of State Dean Rusk that he should arrange face-to-face meetings between US and North Vietnamese officials, and before waiting for a US response had obtained an indication from Hanoi that the communist government would enter into such a dialogue. But Rusk resisted the plan, and this 'put an end to the use of good offices of the Secretary-General in finding a peaceful solution of the Vietnam war' (Nassif, 1988: 50). In 1966 and 1967 U Thant had secret meetings with North Vietnamese officials and in March 1967 sent some proposals to the various parties to the conflict, but they were speedily rejected.

The U Thant years at the UN also witnessed a changing balance between the developed western states and the newly independent states of the third world. In the late 1950s and early 1960s many of the colonies of the western powers emerged into full statehood, which entitled them to UN membership. Of the 51 new members admitted between

1956 and 1968, the vast majority were African, Asian and Caribbean states. Bailey and Daws (1995: 42) noted that by 1961 the Afro–Asian states had obtained a simple majority in the General Assembly, and if they could gain the support of either the western or eastern blocs they could command the two-thirds majority needed to make important decisions.

When these new governments took their seats they brought with them different expectations, value systems and interests. They gave a much higher priority to ending colonialism and to supporting anti-colonial struggles, to fighting racism, and to economic development. As early as 1960 the Assembly passed resolution 1514 which condemned the continuation of coloni-alism and supported the principle of self-determination. A year later a Special Committee was established to monitor the implementation of this Resolution. That same year the US, for the first time since 1951, was unable to defer consideration in the General Assembly of the Chinese representation ques-tion. However, the onset of the Sino–Soviet split in 1960 meant that China now lost the support of the Soviet bloc and the pro-Beijing states could not muster the majority needed to change the status quo.

On the economic front the newly independent third world states formed themselves into the Group of 77 (G-77) in 1964, and through the UN Conference on Trade and Development (UNCTAD) began pressing for a new international economic order more favourable to the newly independent states. Poor states demanded more aid, increased transfer of technol-ogy, debt relief, preferential access to western markets and buffer stocks for key commodities. Many western states dis-trusted these attacks on the liberal/capitalist international economic order and preferred to keep the International Monetary Fund and the World Bank as the main forums to discuss these matters (Robertson, 1969). Here the west had a built-in majority. Another indication of the growing impor-tance of 'developmentalism' at the UN was the creation of the United Nations Development Programme (UNDP) in 1965. The 1970s and 1980s were also designated as development decades, though the impact of this initiative has to be questioned.

In 1965 pressure from the third world also led the UN to increase the number of members of the Security Council from 11 to 15, though the number of permanent members remained the same. The same year the General Assembly passed the International Convention on the Elimination of All Forms of Racial Discrimination (Lerner,1980). With the proliferation of new third world states at the UN, not only could the US no longer rely on a pro-Washington majority within the Organization, but it found itself fighting against a new majority able to pass resolutions which it found objectionable (Tinker, 1977). It was also more difficult for the US to overturn vetoes by other permanent members of the Security Council.

Kurt Waldheim (1972–1981)

Although Kurt Waldheim, the fourth and most controversial Secretary-General, was more activist than his predecessor, like U Thant he was anxious not to antagonize either superpower. However, according to Urquhart (1987: 228), this 'energetic, ambitious mediocrity', although hard working, lacked vision and inspiration and the noble character and integrity of his predecessor. The Austrian diplomat and politician served for two five-year terms between 1972 and 1981. He wanted to serve a third term, but he was prevented from doing so by the threat of a Chinese veto. Subsequent revelations about his war record suggest that he was less opposed to the Nazi regime than he had hitherto indicated (see, for example, Waldheim, 1980: 23–4). In investigations into his past after he failed to be re-elected it was discovered that Waldheim had been placed in the 'A' category by the UN's own War Crimes Commission in 1948. This meant that there was enough evidence against him to bring a prosecution for war crimes (Melvern, 1995: 229).

Waldheim's election coincided with a decline in the Cold War as the superpowers entered a brief period of *détente*. This was characterized by greater co-operation between the two rivals, which led to the signing of arms control agreements between Washington and Moscow (most notably the SALT I Treaty), the end of the Vietnam War and the Helsinki Final Act of 1975. The decline in the East–West conflict led to a temporary growth in interest in North–South divisions, the lingering problems of decolonization, and the racist policies embedded in apartheid.

At the Security Council's first meeting in Africa, at Addis Ababa in February 1972, the Secretary-General was asked to meet with the parties to the Namibian conflict to move forward the process of self-determination in this state, which was ruled by South Africa and so was shackled to an apartheid system. Despite meetings in southern Africa no progress was made. In 1976 the Security Council adopted another resolution which created a framework for the move to self-determination under UN supervision and control. There followed a diplomatic initiative by the five western members of the Council (the Contact Group) which led to a report by Waldheim on how to implement the transition. This plan, submitted in August 1978, envisaged the creation of a mixed military and civilian UN force to be known as the UN Transition Group (UNTAG). However, it was to be nearly ten years before this plan could be implemented because South Africa refused to consider the holding of free elections and because the Namibian conflict became linked to the problems in Angola, especially the presence there of Cuban troops. In 1973 the General Assembly adopted a Convention on the Suppression and Punishment of the Crime of Apartheid (in force in 1976) and in 1974 it barred the South African government from participating in its sessions.

In the summer of 1974 the Cyprus conflict again seized the world's attention when a Greek-sponsored coup against President Makarios provoked a Turkish invasion that led to the *de facto* partition of the island. This could not be prevented by the UN peacekeeping force on the island, though UNFICYP did do important work in helping to arrange local cease-fires, easing the exchange of prisoners, and assisting in the restoration of essential facilities. When the situation stabilized it was immediately clear that UNFICYP had become a 'buffer force' occupying a zone between the Turkish and Greek Cypriot parts of the island.

Although the UN, through its Special Representative, was able to act as a catalyst for intercommunal talks, little progress was made apart from an agreement allowing Turkish Cypriots in the Greek-Cypriot controlled south of the island to move to the Turkish Cypriot north. In January 1977 Waldheim chaired a meeting between the Greek-Cypriot leader Makarios and the Turkish-Cypriot leader Denktash at which some guidelines were agreed. Cyprus would be an independent, non-aligned, federal state with the size of the territory allocated to each group dependent on the economic viability and productivity of the two areas. Continuing UN good offices led to a second document in 1979. The ten-point Kyprianou–Denktash agreement reaffirmed the 1977 approach and stated that priority would be given to certain issues such as the resettlement of Varosha and the adoption of goodwill measures. A final settlement remained elusive and seemed no nearer when Waldheim stood down as Secretary-General in 1982. His successors have had little more success with this most persistent of intercommunal conflicts. Yet Waldheim (1985: 92) claims that the UN's role 'is not one of unmitigated failure' because UNFICYP has 'held the lid on the conflict' and the Special Representative has been 'an essential catalyst and participant in the long succession of intercommunal and international negotiations'.

The Middle East, inevitably, continued to demand the attention of the Secretary-General. Firm US mediation and the dispatch of vast amounts of military hardware to Israel ended the Yom Kippur War of 1973, which had led to an alarming rise in Cold War tensions. The Council had passed Resolution 338 on 22 October which called for a cease-fire and endorsed Resolution 242. Significantly, Resolution 338 was co-sponsored by the US and the USSR, an indication of the crisis management role that the organization could play. The Council also authorized the establishment of two new peace-keeping missions. UNEF II (created on 25 October 1973 by Resolution 340) was to monitor the cease-fire zone between Israel and Egypt, UNDOF (created in May 1974) was positioned on the Golan Heights between Israel and Syria. UNEF's mission ended after the Egyptian–Israeli Agreement of 1979. UNDOF is still in place. As in the case of Cyprus, the UN is frightened that premature withdrawal could disrupt a fragile status quo.

Israeli distrust of the UN remained strong throughout the 1970s, but especially after the PLO leader, Yasser Arafat, was invited to address the Assembly in 1974. The following year the Assembly passed Resolution 3379 which accused Zionism of being a form of racism and discrimination.

In 1978 another UN force was sent to Lebanon. UNIFIL was established in March 1978 by Security Council Resolution 425 after Israel invaded southern Lebanon to prevent Palestinian attacks against its own territory. The mandate of UNIFIL instructed it to confirm the withdrawal of Israeli troops, to restore international peace and security, and to assist the government of Lebanon in ensuring the return of its effective security in the area. However, as Urquhart (1987: 289) has noted, this 'had remarkably little to do with the cruel realities'. After three years of vicious civil war there was no effective government in Lebanon. Furthermore, Israeli troops had no intention of retiring back across the internationally recognised border between the two states, and instead of working with the UN it built up the strength of the Christian militia in the south of the country. Led by Major Haddad, this group frequently engaged in confrontations with UN troops.

In 1982 the Israeli defence forces drove through UN positions on their way to lay siege to Beirut. The UN was not used to monitor the withdrawal of Palestinians from the Lebanese capital that brought the siege to an end. This was performed by a Multinational Force (MNF) composed of US, French and Italian contingents. This, however, got drawn into the

Lebanese conflict and came to be viewed as a hostile presence by certain Islamic groups. Its effectiveness was fatally undermined in a most devastating manner when Islamic fundamentalist suicide bombers killed 241 US marines and 58 French paratroopers on 23 October 1983. The operation collapsed shortly afterwards (Fisk, 1990).

UNIFIL remained in the south of the country where it did have some success in controlling the movement of armed persons and also played a humanitarian role. A comprehensive study by Skogmo (1989) argues that the force helped to stabilize the situation and limit the spread of the conflict. James (1990: 347) agrees that it helped the situation, claiming that 'UNIFIL does seem to have made a significant contribution towards reducing the number of arms, and has thus brought a reasonable measure of security to its exclusive area'.

The decline of East–West confrontation in the early and mid-1970s meant there was more time to focus on North–South issues. In 1973 the developed states pledged to make available 0.7 per cent of their gross national income for development assistance. Yet at the end of the decade Waldheim (1980) was to observe that 'most of them have fallen far short of that quota, and the amount of foreign aid that is received scarcely corresponds with the capacities of the donors'.

The main issue, however, was not aid but a growing demand that the whole economic system be restructured better to meet the needs of third world states. The focus was a call from the G-77 for a New International Economic Order (NIEO). This occurred after the collapse of the postwar Bretton Woods system in August 1971 and the first oil crisis of 1973–4. In 1974 the General Assembly passed the Charter of Economic Rights and Duties of States and special sessions were held in 1974 and 1975 on the theme of a NIEO. However, unrealistic demands for significant structural reforms in the international economic system were largely ignored by the rich world. The North–South relationship became something of a dialogue of the deaf as a result of the growing influence of monetarist, free-market thinking in the US during the Reagan administration. The US remained opposed to the key aspects of the NIEO. The brusque dismissal of the Brandt Report, which supported a global redistribution of wealth, also proved disheartening for supporters of a better deal for the poor states of the world.

The US also rejected the Law of the Sea Treaty, which would have designated some of the world's wealth as the common heritage of humankind. This took eight years to negotiate and Washington had initially supported the talks. However, when the Treaty was completed and the votes were cast in the Assembly, although 130 states voted in favour, the US voted against and many other western states abstained. So, even though the Treaty came into force in 1994, after its sixtieth ratification, most wealthy maritime states have remained unmoved by it.

Other episodes during Waldheim's term as Secretary-General underlined the powerlessness of the Secretary-General in situations where he does not command the support of the great powers. In 1975 the Security Council mandated him to send a special representative to East Timor following the brutal Indonesian occupation of this former Portuguese colony. Skjelsbaek and Fermann (1996: 88) claim that this was a diversion, since many western states did not believe that their interests would be served by putting pressure on Jakarta. Nor was UN involvement possible in the war between Ethiopia and Somalia over the disputed Ogaden region, since the superpowers were offering material support to the opposing sides.

In the Middle East the role of the UN was reduced by both Kissinger and then by President Carter. The UN also played no significant role in the ending of the Vietnam War. Waldheim attended the 1973 Paris talks where the US and North Vietnam agreed a peace treaty, but Urquhart (1987: 232) accepts that the UN's presence was a 'fig leaf'. A Canadian proposal that the UN supervise the cease-fire was quickly rejected. This was largely due to US efforts, though Waldheim notes that in the Middle East case it was the UN who provided the opportunity for the military authorities of Israel and Egypt to meet to discuss issues such as the exchange of prisoners and the separation of forces.

Towards the end of his term of office Waldheim became involved in negotiations to release the 52 American hostages held by the new revolutionary Iranian regime at the US embassy in Tehran. His failure to make progress during a difficult mission to this city led him to observe that

> the Secretary-General of the United Nations is faced with one simple truth: he has no executive power . . . all the chapters of the UN Charter and the principles of international law are of little help if member governments disregard them. (Waldheim, 1985: 11)

Waldheim started his term as Secretary-General when *détente* was at its height. He left it when relations between the superpowers had entered a new period of conflict, competition and distrust. As the global system began to polarize again the United Nations went into significant decline. Many influential members of the new Reagan administration in the US believed that not only did the UN not fit in well with its crusade against communism, but that in some ways it was even anti-American. This we shall examine in the next chapter.

4

FALL AND RISE: THE UN IN THE 1980S

Because he liked to begin each meeting by referring to the one which preceded it, the President [Lyndon Johnson] now reached into the wastebasket and scooped up the notes which the ADA [Americans for Democratic Action] people had brought to the meeting. . . . Then mimicking his previous guests to perfection, he began to read the notes to the assembled chiefs . . . taking particular pleasure in the one that Rauh had written: 'Why doesn't he take the issue of Vietnam to the United Nations?' That one in particular broke them up. (Halberstam, 1992: 573)

This anecdote from the 1960s reminds us of the way in which many policy-makers in the US government viewed the UN during the Cold War. However, in the early 1980s this dismissive attitude increased as opposition to the Organization hardened during the first Reagan administration. By the time the fifth Secretary-General entered office the attacks from Washington were more persistent and damaging.

In his first report on the work of the UN in 1982, the new Peruvian Secretary-General, Javier Perez de Cuellar, spoke of his deep anxiety about international trends (de Cuellar, 1991: 18). He claimed that 'we have strayed far from the Charter in

87

recent years' and that 'we are at present embarked on an exceedingly dangerous course, one symptom of which is the crisis in the multilateral approach in international affairs and the concomitant erosion of the authority and status of world and regional inter-governmental organizations' (de Cuellar, 1991: 6).

Dejection

There were several reasons for this pessimism. In 1982 the Organization had been powerless to stop an Israeli invasion of southern Lebanon, despite the presence of the UN peace-keeping force, UNIFIL. Members of this force could only offer a token and symbolic protest as the Israeli military forces moved through their positions towards their siege of Beirut. Nor was the UN used to monitor the withdrawal of PLO fighters from Beirut. Instead this task was given to the ill-fated Multinational Force (MNF) made up of US, French and Italian contingents. Key parties to this conflict perceived the MNF as a partial body that was supporting the government there. Its impartiality was lost when US forces engaged in large-scale shelling of areas controlled by groups opposed to the government of Lebanon. This led to devastating car-bomb attacks on the US and French barracks in Beirut, which ended any effective role that the MNF was playing. There should have been important lessons here about the importance of peacekeepers maintaining an impartial attitude towards all parties to conflicts.

Although de Cuellar had attempted a mediation initiative during the Falklands/Malvinas conflict the UN was unable to stop this escalating into full-scale war. A Security Council resolution of 3 April which called for a cessation of hostilities and the withdrawal of Argentinian forces was ignored. After the start of fighting the British and US governments vetoed another Security Council Resolution that called for a cease-fire because it was not linked to an Argentinian withdrawal.

The Iran–Iraq War continued oblivious to UN efforts to bring about a cease-fire. Diplomatic efforts to solve the conflicts in Cyprus, Western Sahara, Central America, the Horn of Africa and Afghanistan were no more fruitful. The arms race between the superpowers had restarted, and the US, in line with the 'Reagan doctrine', was fuelling some conflicts by providing economic and military support for groups fighting against communist regimes. 'Time after time', de Cuellar (1991: 17) noted, 'we have seen the Organization set aside or rebuffed'.

De Cuellar was a career diplomat who had been the Peruvian Permanent Ambassador at the UN and a UN Special Representative in Cyprus. In 1979 he became Under-Secretary-General for Special Political Affairs. Once again he was a compromise candidate chosen after China refused to support the re-election of Waldheim, and the US opposed the Tanzanian Selim Ahmed Selim, who had once danced in front of the US Ambassador to the UN, George Bush, after China was admitted to the UN. De Cuellar's time in office as Secretary-General can be divided into two periods that roughly coincide with the dates of his two terms (he was re-elected for a second term in 1986). The first, as already pointed out, began with considerable despondency.

In his 1983 report de Cuellar's concern about international developments continued. He stated that

> The belief in a common future has been, to a large extent, lost in the anxieties of a divided present. Short-term national interests, old resentments and fears, and ideological differences have obscured the vision of the Charter. Concerns for national security or conceived as an open-ended struggle between massive ideological forces seems to have taken the place of the new and enlightened international community envisaged in the Charter. (de Cuellar, 1991: 41)

This was the year that Moscow vetoed a Security Council resolution that attempted to condemn the shooting down of

Korean Airlines flight 007 when it entered Soviet airspace. The same year the US vetoed a Security Council resolution that declared its invasion of Grenada a 'flagrant violation of international law'.

By the mid-1980s there were only four major peacekeeping operations (three in the Middle East and one in Cyprus) and an observer mission in Kashmir; and only in Cyprus was the UN directly involved in the mediation process (Thornberry, 1995: 8). The UN's marginal status found symbolic expression when Reagan and Gorbachev rejected a suggestion by de Cuellar that the first meeting between Reagan and Gorbachev in Geneva should take place in the UN building. At that time the Reagan team saw no political advantage in being linked to the UN, as domestic opinion had turned decisively against it.

The US attitude to the UN

US attacks were spearheaded by the formidable Ambassador to the UN, Jeane Kirkpatrick. The confrontational and unilateralist tone adopted by this new administration did not sit well with the UN's multilateralist style. Waldheim (1985: 177) notes how at his first meeting with the new US president he was informed that the organization was 'heavily biased in favour of the Third World and lacks the moral authority which the world expects from it'.

Of course, the Reagan administration's hostility could draw on a long-standing American disillusionment with the UN. The Organization had always had a troubled relationship with America, where the far right had always regarded it with suspicion. We have already noted in Chapter 3 how American staff working for the Secretariat attracted the attention of the anti-communist witch-hunts during the early Cold War period. The feeling that the UN was full of communists or fellow travellers who were engaged in subversion and espionage against the US was an unquestioned assumption of some American conservatives. De Cuellar (1995: 153) has noted that there were influential members of the Congress who 'acted as if the UN headquarters in New York served mainly as an outpost for the KGB'.

As US influence at the UN declined, more Americans came to adopt a hostile attitude. The admission of Communist China in 1971 attracted especially strong criticism. Kissinger (1979: 785) claims that the reaction in Congress was 'bitter and surprisingly widespread'. The calls for a New International Economic Order, which were viewed as a threat to free-market principles, fuelled US suspicion.

In March 1970 the US used its veto at the Security Council for the first time. By the mid-1970s, according to Stoessinger (1977: vii), the US had 'gone into opposition' at the UN. The US government, for example, opposed the decision by the General Assembly in 1974 to invite Yasser Arafat of the PLO to address them. The US, along with the UK and France, vetoed an attempt by the Security Council to expel South Africa because of its apartheid policies, though the General Assembly still decided to suspend the delegation from Pretoria.

At this time the public face of Washington's resistance was Ambassador Daniel Moynihan. Believing that the US had to 'get its nerve back' and that it had been too ready to adopt a 'retiring role', he began a sustained verbal assault against what he saw as the UN's failure to protect and support civil and political rights. He also objected to the fact that throughout 1974 'UN assemblies were almost wholly given over to assaults on Western positions by combined Communist and Third World blocs' (Moynihan, 1975: 31). He was at the UN in November 1975 when the General Assembly defined Zionism as a 'form of racism and racial discrimination' by 67 votes to 55. In retaliation both Houses of Congress unanimously adopted identical resolutions which opposed any involvement by the US government in the UN Decade to Combat Racism and Racial Discrimination as long as this programme was 'distorted' by the resolution on Zionism. Many believed that

Moynihan's verbal onslaughts against some of the less democratic pro-resolution governments may have alienated third world opinion and increased the anti-Israeli vote.

However, hostility to the UN peaked during the first Reagan administration between 1981 and 1984, spurred on by strong lobbying by influential conservative 'think tanks' like the Heritage Foundation. Gregg (1993: 59) notes that at this point the US 'turned up the heat . . . on the United Nations' and 'undertook to bend UN practice to US political will by playing the most potent card in the US hand – the leverage resulting from the fact that the United States pays 25 per cent of the UN's regular budget'. An immediate target for the new Reagan team was the Law of the Sea Preparatory Commission, which was to set jurisdictions to exploit resources (especially mineral resources on the ocean bed) in the High Seas. Some of these resources were to be designated as the 'common heritage of mankind' and profits made from exploiting them were to be shared with third world states. The Reagan administration took a dim view of such an idea. It argued that such an approach would distort the free market and would work against the interest of US corporations. The US, therefore, refused to ratify the Law of the Sea Convention and refused to fund the Preparatory Commission. The antiregulatory beliefs of the new administration also made it the only state to vote against a WHO resolution that sought to introduce a code for the marketing of powdered baby milk in the third world.

Urquhart (1987: 327) sums up the attitude of the US government at this time as follows:

> Ambassador Kirkpatrick and her chosen associates in the United States Mission seemed to see themselves primarily as embattled defenders of the faith, venturing out from their fortress in the US Mission mostly to do battle with the infidel. . . . They seemed to be more preoccupied with punishing reprehensible behaviour or trying to score points off the Soviet Union.

The US had withdrawn from the International Labour Organization in 1978. In 1982 Washington threatened to review its relations with the IAEA because it was refusing to acknowledge the credentials of the Israeli delegation. This was in response to the destruction of an Iraqi nuclear research reactor by the Israeli airforce in 1981. The same year strong American pressure stopped an attempt by a group of states in the Assembly to expel Israel. Congress then enacted legislation which would withhold funding and US participation from any UN agency which excluded Israel. In December 1983 it signalled its intention to leave UNESCO, pointing to the 'politicization' of this agency and its attempts to establish a new international information order, which could be seen as a threat to independent journalism. Many influential Americans also resented attacks on Israel during UNESCO meetings. On 1 January 1985 the Reagan administration carried out its threat and formally withdrew from UNESCO. The General Assembly also upset US opinion when it condemned the invasion of Grenada as a 'flagrant violation of international law'. Only eight states joined the US in voting against the resolution. In 1985, after the ICJ had decided in November 1984 by 11 votes to five that it had the right to adjudicate a dispute between the US and Nicaragua, the State Department decided to walk away from the proceedings, which focused on the mining of Nicaraguan ports by the CIA. Later that year the White House declared that it would no longer be bound by the compulsory jurisdiction of the Court.

In the same year Congress adopted the Kassebaum amendment, introduced by the Kansas Senator Nancy Landon Kassebaum, who was appalled when the General Assembly authorized the building of a $473 million conference centre in Addis Ababa during the Ethiopian famine (Righter, 1995: 231). This imposed a 25 per cent reduction in the American contribution to the UN budget until the UN system adopted weighted voting on budgetary issues (that is, the US would be given 25 per cent of the votes when budgetary issues were discussed). Opinion in the US seemed to look favourably on this attack on majoritarianism at the UN and accepted the claim that this encouraged irresponsible behaviour from the majority of states who contributed very little to the UN budget. Yet although such a weighted system existed at the IMF and the World Bank, this attempt to introduce it into the UN system as a whole was seen as a fundamental assault on the principle of state sovereignty.

The UN was now in serious financial difficulties and staff morale was at rock bottom. Funding had also been hit by the Gramm–Rudman–Hollings Deficit Reduction Act on Capitol Hill, which required immediate cuts in all federal spending, including funding of the UN. In an attempt to reduce criticism the Assembly adopted resolution 41/213. This ensured that some important budget decisions would have to be made by consensus: in effect giving the US veto powers at a specific point in the budgetary process.

Washington also took unilateral action against the representatives of certain states, who had to obtain entry visas for the US in order to work or visit UN headquarters. In 1986 it ordered the delegations of the USSR, Ukraine and Byelorussia to reduce their staff over the next two years. The following year legislation forced the closure of the PLO mission, a move condemned by the General Assembly. Public antipathy towards the UN was also reflected in the 1987 ABC drama 'Amerika', which showed UN troops occupying the country and blowing up the Capitol as part of a Soviet invasion (Melvern, 1995: 236–7). The same year the former Secretary-General, Kurt Waldheim, was placed on the Department of Justice's 'watch list' and was banned from the US because of his involvement with the Nazis (Melvern, 1995: 235).

Although the government's attitude towards the UN began to improve in 1988, points of tension continued to exist. Washington refused to grant a visa to PLO leader Arafat, who was planning to address the General Assembly on 1 December 1988, because he was deemed to be an accessory to terrorism. However, this was also generally believed to be a violation of legal obligations as set out in the agreement between the host state and the Organization. This Head-quarters Agreement obliges Washington to provide right of entry, transit and residence for anyone attending the UN in New York. Congress did reserve the right to deny entry for reasons of national security, but the vast majority of UN members did not believe that this reservation should have been used to ban Arafat. The Assembly passed a resolution condemning the US and convened in Geneva for three days later in December to allow Arafat to address them. The US, with the UK and France, also vetoed a Security Council resolution that condemned its military intervention in Panama in December 1989, an operation that led to the abduction and trial of President Noriega, a man who had been a CIA 'asset' in the region.

One should not assume that all of the American attacks were unjustified. The UN's own '18-member Group of High-Level Inter-governmental Experts' reported to the Secretary-General in 1986 that the UN was employing too many people at the highest level, and proposed a 15 per cent cut in staff in three years and significant reductions in conferences. However, as the UN moved towards reform hostility from Washington eased, and the changing attitude was also partly helped by the growing reputation of the Secretary-General. In September 1988 Reagan sent his first official invitation to de Cuellar to visit the White House and in September the same year even praised the UN in his address to the General Assembly.

The 'new era'

The 'second Cold War' led to bitter argument between the superpowers at the Security Council and contributed to the general ineffectiveness of the UN during the first de Cuellar term of office. Indeed the Secretary-General admitted that he 'could not point to a single conflict that had been resolved during the five previous years as a result of the UN's efforts' (de Cuellar, 1995: 161). However, for a brief period, as the

Cold War ended more rapidly than anyone had envisaged, it seemed that the US and the UN could work together to create what President George Bush called the 'new world order'. This period of co-operation began with the Namibian operation in 1988, and reached its peak during the Gulf War of 1991. Paradoxically, it was the leader of the other superpower who triggered what Berridge (1991) called the 'return to the UN'.

The UN seemed to benefit from the bewildering and profound changes that occurred in international politics in the second half of the 1980s. One of these changes was the remarkable transformation that the Soviet leader Gorbachev triggered in the Soviet Union. One consequence was the emergence of 'new thinking' about Soviet foreign policy which included a re-appraisal of Moscow's attitudes to the UN. In 1986, for example, the Soviet leader called for a comprehensive system of international security that envisaged a more active role for the UN. In 1988 the Soviet foreign minister, Shevardnadze, suggested to the General Assembly that the UN could create an Environmental Council that would represent all continents.

The Organization, Soviet leaders suggested, could play a more active role in protecting not just the environment, but could also promote human rights and investigate acts of international terrorism. It could make more use of peace-keeping and could have a body to ensure that arms control agreements were kept. The Secretary-General could become more active and the UN could be given an independent fact-finding capability. The Soviet emphasis on multilateralism and international co-operation was favourably compared with the hostile unilateralism of the Reagan administration. However, in the White House a less critical attitude to the UN was emerging as international politics underwent its seismic shift and as the US assessed the costs of unilateralism.

From 1987 onwards the superpowers, cautiously at first, began to co-operate in the Security Council to resolve some of the most persistent problems of the 'second Cold War'. This co-operation began with the Iran–Iraq War. With the en-

couragement of de Cuellar, representatives of the two governments, along with other permanent members of the Security
Council, met informally to consider how this bitter conflict
could be ended. This was complemented by UN mediation to
get the two warring states to accept Security Council resolutions.

Constructive action by the five permanent members had
taken a long time to emerge. The initial inaction of the
Security Council when faced with the blatant Iraqi aggression
that started the war did not impress many observers. Security
Council Resolution 479, passed within a week of its outbreak,
called for a withdrawal of troops to internationally recognised
boundaries, but did not condemn the government of Saddam
Hussein. Some western states were reluctant to take a tough
line against Iraq, even when it began using chemical weapons,
because of geo-strategic considerations. The regime in Baghdad was seen as a counterbalance to Islamic revolutionary
fervour in Iran and the US did not want to give the USSR an
opportunity to exploit poor relations between the west and
Iraq to expand its influence in the region.

Many ineffectual resolutions were passed by the UN during
the war. However, in July 1987 Security Council Resolution
598 demanded by unanimous vote that both parties accept a
cease-fire and withdraw to the 1980 boundaries. This was
accepted by Iraq immediately, but it took another year for
Iran to acquiesce. Policy-makers in Tehran thought that
Resolution 598 was an attempt by the US to prevent an
Iranian victory and the spread of 'Islamic fundamentalism'
further into the Gulf region. In the period after the adoption of
Resolution 598, de Cuellar worked hard behind the scenes
to obtain Iranian support for its cease-fire terms. However,
the key factor which prompted Tehran to abandon their
opposition was that the tide of the war began to turn against
it. A series of military defeats had forced Iranian forces
back almost to the internationally recognised border between
the two states. This made it easier for them to accept Resolution 598.

The Secretary-General declared 20 August 1988 as the date for ending of hostilities and with the cease-fire in place the UN deployed an observer mission, called the United Nations Iran–Iraq Military Observer Group (UNIIMOG), to supervise the cease-fire and the withdrawal of troops to internationally recognised boundaries. Success in the Iran–Iraq War prompted the Secretary-General to remark in his Annual Report for 1988 that with 'the adoption of Resolution 598 (1987) by the Security Council, there has been a reassuring and unanimous interest in restoring the Council's peace-making capacity' (de Cuellar, 1991: 186).

Even more remarkably, the UN was able to play a significant role in the Afghanistan conflict, which was one of the central superpower conflicts of the 1980s. In April 1988 UN Special Representative Diego Cordovez, after six years of effort, was able to obtain the protagonists' signatures on the four documents that comprised the Geneva Accords. In an unprecedented move, the US and the USSR agreed to be co-guarantors of the agreement. The implementation of the Accords was monitored by the United Nations Good Offices Mission for Afghanistan and Pakistan (UNGOMAP). The UN also started a major operation to provide economic and humanitarian assistance to this devastated country. Once again the UN showed how it could help a party, in this case the Soviet Union, save face as it withdrew from an unwanted conflict. Yet although the mission was a success and completed its mandate in March 1990, it did not affect the political situation in Afghanistan and 'the civil war continued unabated after UNGOMAP completed its work' (Birgisson, 1993: 309).

Two other important successes in regional conflicts also increased the prestige of the UN. Both involved substantial UN peacekeeping operations. Indeed, in the Namibian case, for so long a symbol of UN frustration, we see the emergence of what has been termed 'second-generation' peacekeeping. Unlike the 'first-generation' missions, which were almost entirely military affairs concerned with monitoring cease-fires, these new deployments involved the UN in a whole range of complex tasks that needed the skills of civilian and police contingents as well. From this date peacekeeping missions might now be involved in electoral supervision, the disarmament of military units and the training and monitoring of local police forces. Fortna (1993: 372) notes that in many ways 'UNTAG was the first operation of its kind. It was a large composite mission, with a substantial non-military component.'

In December 1988 Angola, Cuba and South Africa signed the Angola/Namibia Accords. According to these documents South Africa would withdraw from Namibia; Cuba would withdraw its forces from Angola, where they were supporting the MPLA government in a civil war against the western-backed UNITA forces; and both South Africa and Angola would co-operate with the Secretary-General to ensure the independence of Namibia through free and fair elections. The Secretary-General was then asked to implement Security Council Resolution 435 and established UNTAG in South West Africa (Namibia). The 8000-strong force was deployed between 1 April 1989 and 21 March 1990 and was mandated to monitor a cease-fire agreement between the South African government and the liberation movement SWAPO; to monitor the borders of Namibia to prevent any infiltration of armed units; and to oversee the elections in November 1989 which led to independence. The operation did not begin well. The creation of UNTAG had been authorized by Security Council Resolution 435 in 1978, during the Secretary-Generalship of Waldheim, so the UN and its member governments had plenty of time to plan its deployment. Yet one of the few criticisms of the force was that UN units were slow in getting to the mission area. In the absence of effective UN supervision SWAPO fighters were able to infiltrate into Namibia against the terms of the cease-fire agreement, which provoked a brutal response by South African forces. For a while it looked as if the entire peace process would collapse.

Nonetheless the UN recovered its position and de Cuellar (1991: 267–8) concluded in his 1990 Report on the Work of the Organization that 'the Namibian experience was a striking demonstration of the results that can be achieved by multilateral effort, by the active engagement of the principle organs of the United Nations and by the members of the Security Council and other states'. It was one of the most successful peacekeeping missions in the history of the UN. James (1990: 268) claims that 'in any analysis of the events which led to Namibia's independence, the tool of international peacekeeping deserves a warm acknowledgement'.

The most ambitious 'second-generation' peacekeeping operation occurred in Cambodia in 1992. The Paris Agreements of October 1991 had opened the way to a peaceful settlement of the civil war in a country plagued for over two decades by severe internal violence complicated by external interventions. Security Council Resolution 718 of 31 October 1991 requested the Secretary-General to prepare a detailed plan to implement these agreements that involved demobilization, the return of refugees and the holding of free and fair elections. The United Nations Force in Cambodia (UNTAC) was deployed in March 1992, shortly after Boutros-Ghali had become the new Secretary-General. It was mandated to verify the withdrawal of foreign forces; to supervise the cease-fire; to take over the administration of the country's defence and public security, foreign affairs, finance and information departments; to monitor the police; to promote human rights; to assist with the repatriation and resettlement of refugees; to facilitate the release of prisoners; to mark minefields; and to organize elections. This involved the deployment of 22 000 military and civilian personnel who were to verify the absence of foreign military forces and the containment and disarmament of the warring factions in their designated areas. This operation cost the UN $26 billion and at its height there was one UN employee for every 400 Cambodian citizens. Up to that date it was by far the largest UN peacekeeping operation.

Opinion remains divided about whether UNTAC should be considered an unqualified success. There were numerous complaints about the conduct and the ability of some of the UN personnel, and the effectiveness of the monitoring of the police and of the human rights situation has been questioned. Ratner (1995), for example, notes that the human rights component was not properly integrated into the operation as a whole. Deficiencies with internal management practices also caused problems, and some civilian peacekeepers were poorly prepared. In some areas the UN was too ambitious and could not implement its mandate effectively. It is also clear that not enough thought was given to how such a large-scale operation would effect the local population and the local economy.

The failure to bring the Khmer Rouge into the peace process continued to blight attempts at peacebuilding in Cambodia. It also meant that the elections did not take place in a neutral and safe environment. Nonetheless Yasushi Akashi, UNTAC's head, did declare them free and fair and 90 per cent of eligible Cambodians did vote between 23 and 28 May, despite some Khmer Rouge intimidation. Therefore the power-sharing government that took power from UNTAC could claim a strong popular mandate. The UN-supervised transition also removed Cambodia as a serious threat to regional stability and opened the way for improved relations between some of the states of South East Asia. Large numbers of refugees returned home. However, developments since the elections suggest that a culture of human rights has still not taken root. In 1997 the First Prime Minister Prince Ranariddh was thrown out of office after a coup by Second Prime Minister Hun Sen.

The UN also deployed a peacekeeping mission to monitor Cuban and Angolan compliance with the commitments they had made in the Angola/Namibia Accords. The United Nations Angola Verification Mission (UNAVEM) was composed of 70 military observers. This task was performed efficiently in uncontroversial circumstances. However, when UNAVEM II was sent to Angola in 1992 to monitor the September elections things did not go so smoothly. This mission was handicapped by its small size (400 observers were meant to cover a state larger than any in western Europe) and a shortage of key materials.

The Central American Peace Process also attracted UN involvement. The United Nations Observer Group in Central America (ONUCA) was deployed in November 1989 by Security Council Resolution 644 to verify that aid to irregular forces and insurrectionist movements had stopped and that the territory of one state was not being used for attacks on its neighbours. The UN was also involved in the elections held in Nicaragua in February 1990. Here the United Nations Observer Mission (ONUVEN) was dispatched to monitor the preparations and holding of free elections – the first time such a peacekeeping operation had been conducted internally in a member state. It was also the first major UN operation in the western hemisphere. A year later the United Nations Observer Mission in El Salvador (ONUSAL) also took the UN into new territory. It was deployed after the San José Agreement between the El Salvador government and the FMLN opposition accepted the need for UN verification of their human rights agreement. The mission tasks included active surveillance of the human rights situation and investigation of specific charges of human rights violations. One commentator has suggested that 'without ONUSAL's active involvement in the implementation of the peace accords, the process would have surely come unstuck' (Hampson, 1996: 97).

The Gulf War and its aftermath

None of these successful tasks undertaken by the UN involved a return to Chapter VII of the Charter: none of these multi-dimensional peacekeeping deployments were collective security operations, and they remained within the ambit of Chapter VI. However, in 1990 a major international crisis erupted when Saddam Hussein of Iraq sent his army into Kuwait. The end of the Cold War meant that the permanent members of the Security Council could now agree on a more forceful international response to this action. Thus, for the first time since the Korean War (1950–3), the Council was able to invoke Chapter VII to undertake military action against a state it deemed to be an aggressor.

As in the case of Korea, the UN did not undertake this military action directly. The Coalition forces saw no need to energise the Military Staff Committee of the UN, made up of the permanent members of the Security Council. Instead the lead role was again taken by the US, acting on the basis of Security Council resolutions. These were pushed through by Washington, partly because many states were genuinely outraged by Iraq's actions, but also because the US government was able to threaten and bribe some members of the Council to take a strong line against Saddam Hussein. Indeed Washington exerted considerable leverage on some reluctant Middle Eastern states to support strong UN resolutions. Egypt's $14 billion debt to the US was written off, Turkey received $8 billion worth of military equipment, and a World Bank loan to Iran was pushed through. The Soviet Union, in internal disarray as it drifted towards terminal collapse, was willing to abandon its support for Saddam Hussein and to accept the Security Council decision to authorize the use of force.

The invasion and annexation of the state of Kuwait by Iraq on 2 August 1990 appeared to many UN members to be a clear breach of the Charter, which prohibits the use of force in interstate relations except in self-defence. Perhaps more importantly, the US and its European allies were concerned that the invasion could destabilize an area of supreme strategic interest to the west. The Security Council responded quickly to the invasion and on 2 August passed Resolution 660, with Yemen abstaining. This demanded that Iraq withdraw, immediately and unconditionally, all its forces from Kuwait. Within the week Resolution 661 invoked Chapter VII to impose mandatory sanctions (Cuba and Yemen abstained).

On 29 November Resolution 678 authorized the Coalition forces to take 'all necessary means' to remove Iraq from Kuwait if Baghdad had not complied with Resolution 660 by 15 January 1991. Cuba and Yemen opposed this resolution and China abstained. The word 'force' was not mentioned in order to appease the Soviet Union, which also insisted that the period up to 15 January be set aside for further negotiation – the so-called 'pause for peace'. However, Moscow did not insist that further authorization would have to be given for the use of force and even though the Resolution does not specifically mention the use of military force, there is no doubt that this was America's intention.

When US military might was applied in early 1991 Iraq suffered a rapid, comprehensive military defeat and the independence of Kuwait was restored. Nonetheless Saddam Hussein remained in power and retained the capability to launch an onslaught on his own Kurdish population after they attempted an uprising in March 1991. This caused a severe humanitarian problem that became an issue of major international concern. Over one million refugees fled to Iran and about 500 000 moved into Turkey. Others were living in the northern mountains of Iraq in appalling conditions. On 5 April 1991 Security Council Resolution 687 condemned the repression of the Iraqi civilian population and insisted that Baghdad allowed immediate access by humanitarian organizations to all of those in need of assistance. Gunter (1992: 7) notes that this was the first occasion that the UN directly addressed the Kurdish issue in Iraq, despite decades of oppression.

Resolution 688 triggered, though it did not directly authorize, 'Operation Provide Comfort', which was undertaken by a coalition of western states. The Resolution did not mention Chapter VII of the Charter, which is the only way that the UN can violate the sovereignty of a state. The UN, as Rosenau (1992: 72) observed, continued to 'honor the sovereignty principle' and many member states would have opposed UN authorization for such an action. China and the USSR, in particular, would probably have vetoed any attempt to initiate direct UN intervention under Chapter VII to protect the Kurdish minority in Iraq, fearful that such an intervention would set a precedent. In the event even the mild and ambiguous Resolution agreed was opposed by Zimbabwe, Cuba and Yemen, with India and China abstaining.

However, whatever its legitimacy, the western coalition created a no-fly zone north of the thirty-sixth parallel to inhibit assaults on the Kurds, and undertook airdrops of food and clothing. In addition six 'safe havens' were established for the Iraqi Kurds, protected by 8000 US, British and French troops, who remained until September 1991. With permission from Baghdad, the UNHCR took control of the humanitarian programme and was protected by 500 UN 'guards'. Basic relief packages and health kits were distributed and attempts were made to encourage refugees to return to their homes. Another no-fly zone was then created south of the thirty-second parallel in Iraq in August 1991 in an attempt to protect the Shiite population from Hussein's wrath.

The Gulf War was fought to expel Iraq from Kuwait. When this goal was achieved the US refused to send its forces into Iraq to remove Saddam Hussein. This stands in direct contrast to the previous case of UN-approved collective security action. As we have seen during the Korean War, when the UN coalition forces had expelled North Korean forces from South Korea, the mandate was changed to allow them to move into North Korea in an unsuccessful attempt to remove the communist regime of Kim Il Sung and reunify the country. No such move was made in the Iraqi case. This, however, presented a problem to the international community, for Saddam Hussein, the man blamed for the Gulf War, was still in power and in control of weapons of mass destruction. In order to try to deal with this perceived threat, UN Security Council Resolution 687, of 3 April 1991 introduced an intrusive set of policies designed to control the behaviour of Iraq in a number of areas. Taylor and Groom (1992: 26) note that these 'required a far more extensive involvement by an international organization in a settlement at the end of a war than had ever been the case'. Johnstone (1994: 1) agrees, claiming that by this Resolution 'unprecedented and far-reaching obligations are imposed on Iraq relating to its border with Kuwait, its weapons of mass destruction, and war reparations.'

Resolution 687, a long document by Security Council standards, requires Iraq and Kuwait to respect their international boundary as determined by a Boundary Demarcation Commission. This was made up of one representative each from Iraq and Kuwait and three independent persons picked by the UN Secretary-General. The Iraqi representative withdrew from the commission in 1992. A UN Iraq–Kuwait Observation Mission (UNIKOM) was established to monitor both a demilitarized zone and the Khor Abdullah waterway between the adversaries, and its mandate was altered in 1993 to allow it to play a deterrence as well as an observation role. Iraq was made liable for the costs that resulted from the invasion and some of its oil income was to be used to pay compensation. Harsh sanctions against Iraq continued even after the end of the war, though the impact of these on Iraqi civilians has provoked some unease in the UN – this despite implementing a procedure to try and alleviate the suffering of Iraqi civilians.

Resolution 687 also attempted to control Saddam Hussein's weapons programmes. Iraq was required to accept unconditionally the destruction of its biological and chemical weapons and was prohibited from developing or acquiring nuclear weapons. Missiles with a range over 150 kilometres also had to be destroyed, keeping Israel out of range. In addition a UN Special Commission (UNSCOM) was created, as a subsidiary body of the Security Council, to inspect installations in Iraq to ensure that these restrictions were upheld. The IAEA was also given an important role and was to have the primary responsibility for nuclear issues. Both UNSCOM and IAEA can make undeclared surprise inspections at any time. Resolution 687 also authorized the use of 'all necessary means' to ensure compliance. This allows states to take military action against Iraq for non-compliance.

The long-term effectiveness of these UN measures is difficult to predict. Only time will tell if Iraq will accept the existing boundary with Kuwait. The impact of economic sanctions is difficult to measure but does not seem to have undermined the resolve of the Iraqi regime. The suffering that these measures are causing for Iraqi civilians is helping to gain some international sympathy for Iraq. The FAO has even quoted an estimate by a Harvard researcher that up to 560 000 children have died in Iraq since the end of the Gulf War because of these sanctions (Stremlau, 1996: 45). Unease about the effect of sanctions encouraged the Security Council to adopt Resolution 986 in April 1995. This allowed Iraq to sell up to $1 billion's worth of oil every 90 days and use the income for humanitarian purposes. However, Iraq objected to the supervisory role given to the UN and resisted for a year until an agreement was reached in May 1996. It also seems likely that Iraq still possesses biological and chemical weapons, including anthrax and other deadly materials, and could quickly acquire a nuclear capability. UNSCOM and IAEA inspectors still do not have full access to all sites in Iraq and there have been many examples of Iraqi obstruction of their work.

There is no doubt that this 'UN action' was really organized and led by the US, for 'as with Korea forty years before . . . the international organization was allowed no part in the management of the 1990/91 crisis and the ensuing 1991 Gulf War' (Simons, 1995: 61). Even after the end of the war the US had the biggest voice in determining UN policy towards Iraq. Most of the drafting of the key Security Council Resolution 687 was done by a 'steering committee' of three of the permanent members who tended to ignore changes to their views suggested by non-aligned states (Johnstone, 1994: 43). During this crisis the permanent members did not go to the full Security Council unless they had reached a consensus on what to do (Taylor and Groom, 1992: 10). The only exception was Resolution 678, which could not obtain Chinese support. The fact that the US played such a prominent role in this enterprise should have induced caution in the minds of those who talked about a new era for the UN.

Inevitably, US influence on the Security Council provoked questions about the UN's impartiality and legitimacy. This perception of bias has been deepened by the Security Council's imposition of partial sanctions against Libya in 1992, which was the result of claims that the regime of Mu'ammar Gadhafi was supporting international terrorism and was, therefore, a threat to international peace and security. The US government claimed that there was Libyan involvement in the bombings of the Pan Am flight over Scotland in December 1988 and the UTA flight over Africa in September 1989. Hundreds of people were killed in these two explosions, though not everyone is satisfied that Libya was involved (see Simons, 1995: 70–7). It was the failure of the Libyan regime to hand over two of its citizens who were suspects in the Pan Am bombing which triggered the imposition of sanctions.

However, at the end of the Gulf War the rhetoric of a new world order seemed to blind many commentators. After all, the most powerful state in the world had co-operated with the most important global international organization to uphold international law. The fact that the international organization was a very junior partner in this operation and that the US was not motivated primarily by legal considerations should have given pause for thought. The Secretary-General, it should be remembered, was humiliated by Saddam Hussein when the former undertook a last-minute peace initiative to Iraq just before the war started in earnest.

Yet after the Gulf War few would have disagreed with the assessment of de Cuellar (1991: 331) in his final report to the Organization in 1991. He claimed that the 'effectiveness of the United Nations can no longer be in doubt'. One indication of this was the rapid increase in the number of peacekeeping operations. Between 1978 and 1988 no new UN peacekeeping missions were created and only three new missions were established between 1966 and 1978. However, from 1988 to

1992 the UN deployed 19 new peacekeeping and observer missions.

So 1991 drew to a close and the UN's international prestige had rarely been higher. This was not just due to the Gulf War. As we have seen, the UN had also helped to end some of the most protracted regional conflicts of the late Cold War years and, in the process, had expanded its repertoire of constructive actions. Indeed, de Cuellar had managed to increase 'remarkably the space of operations for the UN as a whole and the Secretary-General especially' (Dedring, 1992: 167). To do this the UN developed a new pattern of conflict-resolution work that is unique to the UN; a 'special mix' that involved this expanding role of the Secretary-General and 'a complex web of other international movements and interactional patterns' (Dedring, 1992: 162). As if to drive home this point, the outgoing Secretary-General ended his term of office by brokering a peace agreement in El Salvador which ended the 12-year war. The UN was given the task of monitoring the cease-fire and the disarmament and rehabilitation of the guerrilla forces. It also agreed to act as guarantor of the agreements.

As a new Secretary-General entered office at the start of 1992 his Organization appeared to be adjusting well to the post-Cold War era. Public opinion, even in the US, was running in its favour. Many seemed impressed that 'the Security Council showed itself capable of taking decisive action' (Russett and Sutterlin, 1991: 82). Just after the Gulf War one poll in the US found that 70 per cent of Americans had gained respect for the UN (Rosenau, 1992: 56). Many believed that it was moving to a more central position on the global stage.

5

SPREADING DISILLUSIONMENT

A new chapter in the history of the United Nations has begun. . . The new era has brought new credibility to the United Nations. (Boutros-Ghali, 1992–3: 89)

Illusion breeds disillusion. (Boyd, 1962: 20)

The success of the UN in the Gulf War and the positive role that it had played in helping to solve many important regional conflicts following the end of the Cold War led many to believe that there would be a more central place for the Organization in the 'new world order'. So when the Egyptian diplomat Boutros Boutros-Ghali replaced de Cuellar as Secretary-General at the start of 1992 the atmosphere at the UN was unusually optimistic.

Boutros-Ghali had been a law professor at the University of Cairo and an acting foreign minister under President Sadat. He had the strong support of African states and of France (he was educated at the Sorbonne). There was also a feeling that the time had come for the UN to appoint a Secretary-General from Africa. The US government appeared to be suspicious of Boutros-Ghali, and Bush at one point indicated that he wanted the Canadian politician Brian Mulroney to be appointed to the post. Some observers also expressed concern about Boutros-Ghali's age. He was 70 when he began his term of office.

Nonetheless Boutros-Ghali started his new job with considerable vigour and he attempted to keep a promise, made shortly after his election, to implement administrative reform by cutting about a quarter of posts in the UN Secretariat's directorate. He also established an Office of Internal Oversight Service in 1994 to assist the Secretary-General to fulfil his responsibilities in the areas of oversight, management, inspection and evaluation. However, the reform process did appear to many to run out of steam and ultimately did nothing to still the criticisms of the UN's administrative practices. The root-and-branch reform demanded by many in the US failed to materialise.

The same year that Boutros-Ghali took up his post there were 29 full-scale wars in the world and 70 lesser lethal conflicts (Curle, 1995: 44). Nonetheless, he seemed to reflect the new-found optimism at the UN. He began an article in the influential US journal *Foreign Affairs* by stating that a 'new chapter in the history of the United Nations has begun' (Boutros-Ghali, 1992–3: 89) and went on to claim in the next paragraph:

> Along with it have come rising expectations that the United Nations will take on larger responsibilities and a greater role in overcoming pervasive and interrelated obstacles to peace and development.

In January 1992 the first-ever Security Council to meet at the level of heads of state and government, itself an indication of the higher status accorded to the Organization, asked Boutros-Ghali to offer an analysis of ways of strengthening the UN in the realm of international peace and security. In the middle of 1992 he responded with a definitive statement about the role of the UN in the post-Cold War world. Entitled *An Agenda for Peace*, it was an optimistic and, in places, imaginative document, especially when it addressed the UN's prevention and *peacebuilding* roles. It envisaged a greater use of peace-enforcement, but it also seemed to blur the distinction between the two when it described peacekeeping as the deployment of a UN presence in the field '*hitherto* with the consent of all the parties concerned' (emphasis added). Without consent peace-keeping would slide into the much more difficult terrain of peace-enforcement, as the UN was to find in Bosnia and Somalia.

In support of his call for a stronger UN role the new Secretary-General mentioned the growth in UN peacekeeping operations, the broadening of the role of peacekeepers and the possibility that the UN could, post-Gulf War, be a credible agent of collective security. First- and second-generation missions continued to grow. In 1992 the 400 electoral observers that made up the United Nations Angola Verification Mission (UNAVEM) were deployed to monitor the ill-fated elections that were meant to end the long-standing civil war there. However their small number made it difficult for the UN to refute with any credibility the accusation from the defeated party that the election had been a fraud. Nonetheless the need for a UN presence to assist post-violence reconstruction was recognised when, despite the shortcomings of UNAVEM II, a new peacekeeping force was established by Security Council Resolution 976. From February 1995 until June 1997, UN-AVEM III continued to help this tormented state in a number of ways. It provided good offices and mediation; monitored the extension of the administration throughout the country and the process of national reconciliation; supervised the cease-fire; assisted in the establishment of quartering areas for the rebel UNITA forces and the movement of government troops to barracks; supervised the collection of the weapons of UNITA; verified the free circulation of persons and goods; monitored the Angolan National police; co-ordinated and supported humanitarian activities. UNAVEM also declared formally that the conditions for free and fair presidential elections were fulfilled and verified and monitored the electoral process.

This sort of work, designed to help societies coming out of conflict, was also undertaken elsewhere. The UN Observer

Mission to Verify the Referendum in Eritrea (UNOVER), established in 1993, smoothed the transition to full Eritrean independence. In the same year the UN Operation in Mozambique (UNOMOZ) was deployed after the General Peace Agreement signed in Rome to help return this war-torn state to peace and democracy. It helped to conduct free and fair elections in October 1994 and was withdrawn in early 1995. The United Nations Observer Mission in Liberia (UNOMIL) was established, also in 1993, to work with the Economic Organization of West African States' 'peacekeeping force' (called ECOMOG) to help implement the Cotonou Agreement.

The Organization also helped to prepare the ground for a referendum on the future of Western Sahara through the work of the UN Mission for the Referendum in Western Sahara (MINURSO). A key task is to identify potential voters in a situation where the main parties disagree about who is eligible to vote. This has ensured a slow process and has delayed implementation of the UN referendum plan. Finally, one should note the work of the United Nations Verification Mission in Guatemala (MINUGUA), which is undertaking verification and institution-building activities to help the peace process there. Human rights monitors are attached to this force.

By the end of June 1994 there were 17 active peacekeeping operations, using over 70 000 troops and costing about $3 billion a year. Between 1945 and 1991 the Security Council authorized the use of force only twice for purposes other than self-defence. Between 1991 and mid-1994 Chapter VII was used to authorize the use of force five times (the Gulf, Somalia, former Yugoslavia, Rwanda, Haiti). In addition, between January 1992 and September 1993 over one hundred missions of representation, goodwill and fact-finding were deployed on behalf of the Secretary-General. Many states also received some form of electoral assistance. Indeed, in 1992 an Electoral Assistance Division was established at the UN to facilitate this work.

Diplomatic activity inevitably increased in New York as a result of the growing significance of the Organization. The report *Our Global Neighbourhood* (Commission on Global Governance, 1995: 236–7) points out that from 1946 to 1989 there were 2903 Security Council meetings that resulted in 646 Resolutions, an average of about 15 Resolutions a year. From 1990 to mid-1994 there were 495 meetings and 288 Resolutions, an average of over 70 a year.

However, the large-scale 'peace-enforcement' operations in Bosnia and Somalia, authorized by Chapter VII of the Charter, demonstrated the limitations of the UN's role. The failure of the UN to stop the genocide in Rwanda in 1994 added to a growing chorus of criticism directed at the Organization. As a result, during the UN's fiftieth birthday celebrations in 1995 the Organization was on the defensive. The optimism of the early 1990s had evaporated in the face of what Ramsbotham and Woodhouse (1996) have termed 'international-social conflict', that is, conflicts that are rooted in relations between communal groups but which cause massive human suffering and become a crisis for the state and for the interstate system. Whereas many of the successes of the late 1980s had been in conflicts that were left over from the Cold War, these new eruptions of violence seemed rooted in the new realities of the post-Cold War world, and the UN seemed unsure about how to deal with them.

The former Yugoslavia

The UN involvement in the former Yugoslavia began conventionally enough in Croatia with the deployment of a peacekeeping force. This followed an agreement between the Croats and the Croatian Serbs mediated by the Secretary-General's personal envoy, Cyrus Vance. In response the Security Council passed Resolution 743 which approved the creation of the UN Protection Force (UNPROFOR) for a period of 12 months. In Croatia it was deployed into the UN

Protected Areas (UNPAs). These were the parts of Croatia where the Serbs were in the majority and where the Yugoslav army was dug in to protect them. Under the Vance agreement the UN was to replace the Yugoslav army and the UNPAs would be demilitarised. Ironically, the headquarters for UN-PROFOR was to be Sarajevo, the capital of Bosnia and Herzegovina, because it was felt that this would be safer than locating it in Croatia itself.

However, the situation in Bosnia deteriorated after the referendum in February 1992, which produced a majority in favour of independence. The result did not settle the conflict there because the elections were boycotted by Bosnian Serbs who, with the support of the Serbian government in Belgrade, wanted a 'Greater Serbia' to include parts of Bosnia. So they proclaimed their own Republic with a capital in Pale and refused to accept the legitimacy of the new government in Sarajevo. Despite this internal division, Bosnia was admitted to the UN in May, though by this time a bitter civil war was under way.

The civil war caused a massive humanitarian problem that pricked the conscience of the international community. With humanitarian agencies finding it hard to operate in a war zone, the Security Council authorized UNPROFOR to take control of Sarajevo airport to ensure a proper flow of aid. On 13 August Security Council Resolution 770 extended the mandate of the UN force to include ensuring the delivery of humanitarian assistance throughout Bosnia and Herzegovina. In so doing it invoked Chapter VII of the Charter.

After the deployment of UNPROFOR in both Croatia and Bosnia the mandate of the force was constantly altered. There were over 60 Security Council Resolutions on the former Yugoslavia between September 1991 and July 1994. In Croatia, for example, UNPROFOR was given additional tasks: monitoring the 'pink zones' (Serb areas outside the UNPAs); controlling entry into the UNPAs; monitoring the demilitarization of the Prevlaka Peninsula; and control of the Peruca dam. As a result operations became more complex, which led to more and more demands on UN personnel. Some of these the UN was clearly ill-prepared for.

As the situation in Bosnia and Herzegovina deteriorated, the UN imposed sanctions on the Federal Republic of Yugoslavia (that is, Serbia and Montenegro) in May 1992 in Security Council Resolution 757. A year later Resolution 820 also prohibited the transfer of all goods through Yugoslavia and allowed the freezing of Yugoslav funds held overseas. All commercial traffic was also banned within the territorial waters of Yugoslavia. A no-fly zone in Bosnia was declared in October 1992 by Council Resolution 781, though this was consistently ignored by the Serbs.

In April 1993 the UN began to adopt a 'safe areas' policy, beginning with the town of Srebrenica and its surroundings (Security Council Resolution 819). The policy was then expanded to include Bihac, Gorazde, Sarajevo, Tuzla and Zepa (Security Council Resolution 824). This can be interpreted as an admission that the UN could not protect the population of Bosnia as a whole and that its personnel might only be able to defend people at risk within designated zones. UN forces were authorized to use military force against any attack on these areas that threatened UN personnel, but member states were not willing to offer enough troops to UNPROFOR to make this policy effective.

Force was sometimes used by NATO, though the UN allowed many Serb attacks to go unpunished. This was especially true for Sarajevo, where the international media was based; but attacks by Serbs on other safe areas also damaged the credibility of the Organization. It also led to embarrassing disagreements between different UN members and between the UN and NATO about the advisability of air strikes as retaliation for these attacks. These were especially strong during the Serb shelling of Bihac in late 1994. This was chosen as a Serb target partly because it was protected by a UN contingent from Bangladesh (that is, non-NATO).

The reaction to the Bihac shelling exposed the divisions on the Security Council about how to react to such provocation.

The British, fearing for the safety of its troops serving with UNPROFOR and not wanting to disrupt negotiations, argued for a less hard-line response to the Bosnian Serbs than either the US or France. Russia adopted the most pro-Serb attitude for cultural and political reasons. There are also indications that by the middle of 1995 senior UN officials believed that the UN should withdraw from the three eastern safe havens of Srebrenica, Gorazde and Zepa, despite the assurances given in Resolution 819. Frustration with the UN increased in May 1995 when Serbs seized UN personnel to act as hostages when NATO air strikes destroyed an arms dump near Pale.

In 1994 the UNPROFOR operation in Croatia was renamed the United Nations Confidence Restoration Operation (UNCRO). A cease-fire agreement between the government and the Serb authorities in Croatia in March 1994 allowed UNCRO to monitor the forward troop deployment lines and verify that all weapons systems specified in the agreement were deployed as agreed. The force also manned checkpoints at crossing points into the UNPAs and UN civilian police were meant to supervise the local police. After a further agreement in December 1994 UNCRO was also given a mandate to advance the process of reconciliation and the restoration of normal life. This included the implementation of humanitarian measures and the opening of transportation networks. Other tasks given by the Security Council included support for confidence-building measures, the monitoring of human rights, the monitoring of traffic crossing international frontiers at designated crossing points, the monitoring of the demilitarization of the Prevlaka Peninsula and the facilitation of the return of refugees (UN Doc. S/1995/320).

However, the UN in Croatia had always been caught between contradictory expectations. The government in Zagreb wanted UNCRO to allow Croats to return to their homes and to re-establish the authority of the Croatian government. Serbs wanted the force to offer protection until it could consolidate a separate administration. President Tudjman of Croatia had always regarded the special status of the UNPAs and the 'pink zones', and therefore the need for a UN presence, as a temporary obstacle on the road to the reunification of his country. He was concerned that the longer the UN remained in place the greater legitimacy would be accorded to these Serb-controlled areas of Croatia. In Zagreb this was sometimes called the 'Cypriotization' of the conflict.

The UN was unable to broker an agreement between the Croats and Serbs in Croatia, and when the Croatian government finally moved against the UNPAs in 1995 UNCRO was unable to stop it. In January 1995 President Tudjman had threatened to expel UNCRO. In May he showed that the continuing presence of the UN force was not a major obstacle to his plans. When the Croatian army regained control of the UNPA of Western Slavonia (an area the UN referred to as 'sector west') all UNCRO could really do was supervise the evacuation of Serbs who wished to leave the region after a cease-fire agreement on 3 May. Then at the start of August 1995 Croatian government forces seized control of a second UNPA in the Krajina, creating 200 000 refugees. Once again the UN was powerless to act. After the collapse of two of the three UNPAs and the exodus of refugees that followed, UNCRO's mission ended in January 1996 though a new United Nations Mission of Observers in Prevlaka (UNMOP) was established to monitor the demilitarization of the Prevlaka Peninsula. A United Nations Transitional Administration for Eastern Slavonia, Baranja and Western Sirmium (UNTAES) was also set up to facilitate demilitarization in these areas and to oversee the voluntary return of refugees and displaced persons. Its civilian component was given a mandate to establish and train a temporary police force, restore the normal functioning of public services, monitor human rights and organize elections for local government bodies.

The credibility of the safe areas policy in Bosnia finally collapsed with the Bosnian Serb capture of Srebrenica in July 1995. The 400-strong Dutch UN contingent watched helplessly as Bosnian Serb forces took the town after senior UN officials stopped an air strike against Serb targets that could have provided some protection to both Bosnian Moslems and UN troops in this besieged city. This was followed by the massacre of thousands of Bosnian Moslem men by Bosnian Serbs. The safe area of Zepa fell to Bosnian Serbs three days later, creating about 10 000 refugees. Gorazde also appeared to be under imminent threat, as did Sarajevo. At the end of August, 37 people were killed when a shell, presumed to have been fired by Serbs, landed on the Bosnian capital.

By now the western powers had taken enough. Frustrated by the cautious approach adopted by the UN Special Representative Yasushi Akashi, the UN was sidelined as NATO instituted 'Operation Deliberate Force' from 30 August to 4 September. This was accompanied by demands that the Bosnian Serbs respect a 20km exclusion zone around Sarajevo for heavy weapons, cease their attacks, and allow access to the airport and roads into and out of the city. A Rapid Reaction Force was also created that was less amenable to direct UN control.

The Dayton/Paris Agreement at the end of 1995 brought to an end the UN's lead role in Bosnia. After several notable failures by the European Union/UN negotiating teams, the US was able to broker a peace agreement. It replaced UN-PROFOR with a 60 000-strong force under NATO leadership. Of these, 20 000 came from the US, and 4000 came from Russia. This deployment went under the name of Peace Implementation Force (I-FOR), was more heavily armed than UNPROFOR, and its rules of engagement were much broader. It was meant to stay in Bosnia for only one year, but it still remains in place, under its new name of S-FOR. The last vestiges of UN control were swept away at a meeting in London held in December 1995. The old UN-led International Conference on Former Yugoslavia was abolished and a new Peace Implementation Council was created. This was endorsed by the Security Council even though the UN was not given a seat on its Steering Board.

However a smaller UN presence remained in Bosnia through the United Nations Mission in Bosnia and Herzegovina (UNMIBH). This was composed of an International Police Task Force (IPTF) and a civilian office. The IPTF was mandated by Security Council Resolution 1035 of December 1995 to monitor and inspect law enforcement activities, train and advise law enforcement personnel, and to assess threats to public order. The mandate of the force was extended to June 1998 at the end of 1997.

Any overall assessment of the role of the UN in Yugoslavia has to put some items in the plus column. The Organization was able, despite some serious military obstacles, to deliver humanitarian supplies to hundreds of thousands of civilians in desperate need, especially during the bitter winters. In Macedonia it created the first-ever 'preventive peacekeeping force', which was deployed along the borders with Albania and Yugoslavia. Security Council Resolution 795 of December 1992 authorized it to monitor the border areas and report any developments that could threaten Macedonia.

However, UNPROFOR was not able to stop serious fighting when one or more of the parties wanted it, nor could it protect people from serious human rights abuses, including genocide and 'ethnic cleansing'. In Bosnia its 'safe havens' policy collapsed into a tragic farce in Srebrenica. Some have questioned the morality of a policy which could not deter Serb aggression but which denied Moslems the arms to defend themselves. Ignatieff (1995: 31) claims that the policy of the west was 'we will not fight the chief aggressor, and we will not enable the victim to resist; but we will try to prevent the victims from being wiped out'. The UN's own Special Rapporteur in the former Yugoslavia for the commission on human rights, Tadeusz Mazowiecki, even resigned in protest at UN policy. He claimed that 'UN structures are not geared to monitoring or counteracting human rights abuses' and argued that 'the UNPROFOR mandate was essentially sick' because 'it was assumed that it was possible to go into a war situation with a peacekeeping mandate' (Mazowiecki, 1995: 71).

The UN operation was also unsettled by tensions between the UN and NATO and between the permanent members of the Security Council. Public statements by senior UN personnel also reveal deep divisions within UNPROFOR and doubts about the ability of the UN bureaucracy to command, control and support peacekeeping forces in the field (see, for example, MacKenzie, 1994).

Supporters of the UN claim that it was able to do a limited but important humanitarian job in a situation where there was no will from the powerful members of the Organization to provide the military power needed to try to stop gross violations of human rights. However, the memories that will be longest to fade are the negative ones: the unending siege of Sarajevo, the Omarska concentration camp, UNPROFOR's quick exit from Srebrenica, and the sight of kidnapped UN personnel used as human shields to protect Bosnian Serb positions.

Haiti

In September 1991 a military coup removed from power the democratically elected government of President Aristide of Haiti. This act was condemned by the Organization of American States (OAS), which adopted a resolution demanding his immediate reinstatement. In 1992 the General Assembly added its condemnation in Resolutions 46/7 and 47/20 and a UN special envoy was appointed by Boutros-Ghali to participate in a mission to Haiti. The next year a joint UN and OAS International Civilian Mission (MICIVIH) to Haiti was planned to monitor the human rights situation there. The Security Council also imposed an oil and arms embargo against Haiti in Resolution 841 of June 1993. Under this pressure the leader of the coup, Cedras, signed an agreement with Aristide that committed both parties to a political dialogue under UN and OAS auspices. This led to the New York pact of July 1993 in which the parties agreed to uphold human rights and refrain from actions that would undermine the transition to democracy. Aristide was to appoint a new Prime Minister.

The agreement encouraged the Security Council to suspend the sanctions against Haiti after the Haitian parliament had ratified Aristide's choice of Robert Malval as Prime Minister. In August 1993 Boutros-Ghali recommended sending 567 Civpol and 60 military trainers to the island and this was approved in principle by the Security Council in Resolution 862, when it authorized the dispatch of an advance force to prepare for a possible UN mission. On 23 September the Security Council adopted Resolution 867 which created the UN Mission in Haiti (UNMIH). This was to establish a new police force and help to modernize the Haitian military. However, when an attempt was made on 11 October to land UNMIH personnel at Port-au-Prince armed civilians prevented them from leaving their ship, the *Harlan County*. So the Security Council re-imposed the oil and arms embargo and the following year added new items to the list of sanctions. This could not hide the fact that this was a humiliating situation for the UN, which had found its own plans frustrated by an armed mob.

In July 1994 Security Council Resolution 940 invoked Chapter VII to authorize the creation of a multinational force under unified command to use 'all necessary means' to remove the existing government in Haiti and restore legitimate government. Sixty UN monitors would observe the actions of this force and prepare for UNMIH's deployment. This Resolution also expanded UNMIH's mandate to include: assisting the legitimate government of Haiti to sustain the secure and stable environment created by the multinational force; professionalizing the Haitian armed forces; and, with the OAS, assisting in establishing an environment conducive to the organization of free and fair elections. In September President Clinton reported that since all diplomatic efforts to resolve the situation had been exhausted force could be used to implement Resolution 940. Worried by this prospect, the regime held talks with former President Jimmy Carter and agreed to resign if a general amnesty was granted to the Haitian parliament and the leaders of the old regime were allowed to stay in the country. On 19 September the first contingents of the multi-national force landed on the island, followed by UNMIH personnel. The following month President Aristide returned and in April 1995 the US president handed over control of the peacekeeping operation to the UN.

In June 1996 UNMIH came to an end, though new UN missions were created to carry on some of its tasks. The United Nations Support Mission in Haiti (UNSMIH) was deployed between June 1996 and July 1997 to help with the professionalization of the police and assist in the maintenance of a secure and stable environment. The United Nations Transition Mission in Haiti (UNTMIH) also helped to contribute to the professionalization of the police between August and November 1997, whilst in December 1997 the United Nations Civilian Police Mission in Haiti (MIPONUH) took over this task. As in the case of Cambodia, although the UN had played a role in the transition to democratic government, doubts exist as to whether a democratic culture has taken root on the island. The way that a small clique of dictatorial leaders were able to defy the UN for so long also called into question the effectiveness of the organization.

Somalia

After the overthrow of the Somali ruler Said Barre in 1991 numerous factions, based around clans, battled for political power. The conflict was concentrated in the southern part of the country where the two main factions, different lineages of the Hawiye clan, competed for power. One was led by Mohamed Farah Aideed of the Hawiye Habr Gedr and the other was headed by Ali Mahdi Mohamed from the Hawiye Abgal. They had been at war with each other since October 1991, when Aideed had withdrawn his recognition of the provisional government of Ali Mahdi. The absence of any central authority contributed to a humanitarian crisis in which millions of Somalis were at risk from malnutrition.

In January 1992 Security Council Resolution 733 called for an arms embargo on Somalia. This was far too late to have an influence on a country already overflowing with weapons. The same month a senior UN official, James Jonah, visited Mogadishu and made Aideed suspicious that the UN was tilting towards his enemy, Ali Mahdi. Drysdale (1997: 120) claims that 'Aideed's perception of Jonah's diplomacy was that it fell short of even-handedness, appearing to give unreserved recognition to Mahdi as interim president'. Nonetheless meetings involving the warring parties were held under UN auspices, and this did result in a temporary cease-fire from March 1992. This opened the way for the deployment of the United Nations Operation in Somalia (UNOSOM I), mandated by Security Council Resolution 751 of April 1992 to monitor the cease-fire in the Mogadishu area. Mahdi approved the deployment of this force, but the consent of Aideed was not forthcoming. In July the Secretary-General increased the size of UNOSOM with the addition of 500 Pakistani troops who were sent to protect relief workers and ensure the delivery of aid.

Nonetheless, by the end of the year it was clear that this small UN force could not carry out its mandate. For weeks it hardly ever left its barracks and was far too inconsiderable to perform the tasks given to it. To add to the UN's problems its special envoy in Somalia, Mohammed Sahnoun, resigned in October because of disagreements with the UN hierarchy and worries about the interventionist position of the Secretary-General, who was now prepared to send in more troops without the consent of the warring parties. In contrast to this approach, Sahnoun had been pursuing a policy based on a respect for local culture, an emphasis on consensus and extensive contacts with traditional authority structures in Somalia, especially the clan elders. His doubts about the role of the UN eventually spilled over into a public disagreement between Sahnoun and Boutros-Ghali. Sahnoun remained unapologetic about his public criticisms, arguing that the UN 'is not a secret organization, it is normal that people should say when there are serious shortcomings with terrible consequences for lives'(*Guardian*, 25 November 1992).

On 28 August, Security Council Resolution 755 authorized the Secretary-General to increase the size of UNOSOM to protect relief workers and ensure the delivery of aid. An extra 3500 troops were allocated but opposition from some warlords delayed their deployment. Frustrated by the continuing inability to deliver aid in conditions of relative safety some NGOs working in the field appealed to President Bush who, in the twilight of his presidency, agreed to add the weight of the Pentagon to the UN operation.

By the end of the year the humanitarian problem had become desperate. Makinda (1993: 11) described a situation where 'Somalia has no army, no police force, no civil service, no banking system and no schools or hospitals that function'. The situation was further complicated when the Issaq clan in northern Somalia declared an independent 'Republic of Somaliland'. However, the UN has refused to confer any legitimacy on this entity and has continued to regard it as part of the Somali state.

Towards the end of 1992 it was claimed by the UN that two million people were at risk from malnutrition and that 80 per cent of aid was being seized by the warlords. Estimates about the extent of the emergency vary, but according to one calculation about 3000 people were dying every day (Ramsbotham and Woodhouse, 1996: 206–9). Airlifts of food and other supplies conducted by the US and other western states were unable to match the scale of the emergency. So on 3 December Security Council Resolution 794, invoking Chapter VII of the Charter, created the United Task Force on Somalia (UNITAF). This legitimized the US-led operation called 'Restore Hope'. This 37 000-strong force took a more robust attitude and was authorized to use all necessary means to create a secure environment for the safe delivery of humanitarian aid. It was not an exclusively US operation since over twenty states participated.

In one sense it did accomplish its mandate. Humanitarian aid was delivered with greater efficiency than before. The looting of supplies stopped. Deaths from malnutrition dropped, though there is still disagreement whether this was mainly because of the UN presence or because the famine had already peaked in the previous months. However, no solution to the inter-clan conflict was forthcoming. UN efforts to broker a cease-fire at meetings in Addis Ababa in January and March of 1993 failed when Aideed claimed that other parties had resumed fighting. Other meetings, such as the ill-fated Mudug Conference in June 1993 (which the UN at first backed and then refused to support), the Kismayu Conference of February 1994, and the Nairobi Conference in May 1994 were all unable to find a sustainable settlement.

Nor was any attempt made to disarm the factions. This was an issue that caused some friction between the Secretary-General and the US government. Boutros-Ghali wanted a tough line and argued that this disarmament was implied in the mandate of the force which instructed it to create a 'secure environment'. However, Washington did not want UNITAF to take on this role and therefore opted for a narrow inter-pretation of the mandate. This was the approach adopted by the US commander of UNITAF, Lieutenant General Robert Johnston, and special envoy Robert Oakley, who had been US ambassador in Somalia and was able to establish a working relationship with both Mahdi and Aideed. The narrow ap-proach was preferred because the US was anxious not to do anything that would prolong or complicate UNITAF's mis-sion. It wanted the more complex and difficult tasks to be left to the follow-up UN mission. Here we see another indication, perhaps, of the UN's usefulness as an organization to pass bucks to. However, it should be noted that this non-confronta-tional approach on the issue of disarmament reduced the hostility to international intervention that had developed in the Aideed camp and allowed UNITAF to operate in a situation of relative peace.

In May 1993 the US withdrew most of its troops against the wishes of the UN, though it retained a Quick Response Force in the area, capable of attacking targets with helicopter gunships and special forces. Security Council Resolution 813 then established UNOSOM II, under UN command. It was given a mandate to 'maintain the cease-fire, facilitate the delivery of humanitarian supplies, and create conditions conducive to a political settlement' (Makinda, 1993: 76). However, it got drawn into a serious confrontation with General Aideed, leading to the deaths of UN personnel and Somalis. Twenty-six soldiers were killed on 5 June 1993 after the Pakistani contingent had entered a radio station defended by supporters of Aideed. In response the Security Council passed Resolution 837 which authorized the UN to use force to ensure the arrest and detention of those responsible for attacks on the UN. This was viewed by the Aideed faction as a declaration of war and it only served to increase tensions between Aideed's supporters and UNOSOM II. On 12 June UN forces retaliated and killed about 100 Somalis, including women and children. The next day Pakistani UN troops opened fire on unarmed protesters, killing 20. On 17 June Aideed's forces killed five more UN troops, one from Pakistan and four from Morocco. Another two Pakistani soldiers were killed at the end of June and three Italian members of UNOSOM II died on 3 July. In the same week six local UN civilian employees were killed.

The incident which had the greatest impact, however, occurred on 3 October 1993. On this day 12 US soldiers were killed and 75 were wounded when they attempted to seize two Aideed aides. Pictures of their dead bodies being dragged through the street by a jubilant crowd had a profound impact on US opinion and undermined support for the whole Somali operation. Between 200 and 1000 Somalis were also killed in this battle. Woods (1997: 165) points out that President Clinton 'immediately abandoned the ongoing policy and adopted a policy looking to minimize any further casualties while seeking a formula for early US withdrawal'. Washington

announced that US troops would remain to support UNO-
SOM only until 31 March 1994.

In the absence of any significant move towards a negotiated
settlement, and with no clear objectives before it, UNOSOM
II limped along for another year, but was withdrawn in
March 1995. Weiss (1995a: 172) remarked that at the time
of withdrawal, not only was there no political settlement in
sight, but the 'warring parties are rested, better armed, and
ready to resume civil war'. Bruce Clarke (1995), in an article
in the *Financial Times*, talked about the 'whimpering retreat
from Mogadishu'. Makinda (1993: 89–90) concluded an analysis of the Somali case by stating that it showed 'how
inadequately equipped the international system is to deal
decisively with humanitarian problems' and that the UN
action was 'unprecedented both in scale and cost, but there
is nothing to suggest that it is a viable model for international
responses to massive humanitarian disasters'.

The Clinton administration and UN peacekeeping

One reason for concentrating on the Somali case is that it had
a major impact on US attitudes to the UN. After the withdrawal from Mogadishu the Clinton administration reassessed
its whole attitude to UN operations. According to Johnston
and Dagne (1997: 196–7) the 'Somalia operation did not have
broad-based support in Congress' at the start of the operation,
but as the situation deteriorated even its limited support began
to erode. As a result, the same authors claim that this episode
'fundamentally changed the course of US foreign policy'
(Johnston and Dagne, 1997: 202).

In May 1994 Presidential Decision Directive 25 confirmed
that Washington was now adopting a more cautious attitude to
UN peacekeeping and enforcement operations. It stated that
the US did not support the idea of a standing UN army or
proposals to earmark US units for UN operations. It also
pointed out that the President would never relinquish com-

mand of US forces, though it might place them under the operational control of a foreign commander. The document seemed to suggest that the US would, in future, support only well-defined peace operations that would provide 'finite windows of opportunity' to allow combatants to end their conflicts. Seventeen preconditions were set out for US involvement in UN missions. The President insisted that peace operations should not be open-ended and each mission should have a specified time-frame, an integrated political/military strategy, a firm budget estimate and specified troop levels. Command and control arrangements had to be adequate, domestic support had to exist and US participation would only be allowed if this was necessary for an operation's success. There should also be realistic criteria for ending the operation. The National Security Revitalization Act the following year also allowed Congress to impose even more restrictions on US participation.

These new restrictive guidelines were adopted to shape US policies just at the time when the UN was experiencing perhaps its greatest failure in Rwanda. The 'Somalia syndrome', based on a desire not to cross the 'Mogadishu line' or to allow 'mission creep', was to have a devastating impact on the UN's ability to respond positively to the Rwanda crisis. This was a significant volte-face in US policy and 'only three years separate the bullish optimism of that guaranteed survival to the Kurds in northern Iraq and the utter indifference to Rwanda's genocide in April 1994' (Weiss, 1995b: 228). Now, not only was the US government opposed to direct US involvement and the 'aggressive multilateralism' of the early 1990s, it also wanted to restrain UN involvement in general in case the US military would be forced to organize I-FOR-type missions to rescue failed UN peacekeeping operations.

Rwanda: Observing genocide

The former Belgian colonies of Burundi and Rwanda have been bound together in a bitter cycle of mass murder for generations. Prunier (1995: 198) notes how their 'past histories, their compatible social structures, their constant and almost obsessive mutual scrutiny, fated them to be natural mirrors of each other's hopes, woes and transformations'. Between 1959 and 1962 the Hutus in Ruanda–Urundi killed thousands of Tutsis, who had been the dominant group for centuries. Up to 70 per cent of Tutsis may have left between 1959 and 1964 (Manikas and Kumar, 1997: 64). In 1962 Rwanda and Burundi were created out of this Belgian colony, with the Hutus in power in Rwanda and the Tutsis still in control in Burundi. In 1972, 150 000 Hutus died in Burundi in massacres organized by extremist Tutsis. Tutsis were killed, in turn, in the violence this triggered in Rwanda. In 1973 the Hutu General Habyarimana came to power in Rwanda after a *coup d'état* and his regime remained stable until 1990, when the Tutsi Rwandan Patriotic Front (RPF) launched an invasion from neighbouring Uganda. This was repelled, with help from France and Belgium, and thousands of Tutsi and Hutu 'collaborators' were murdered in the reprisals that followed. In 1993 the first Hutu President of Burundi, Melchior Ndadaye, was killed by Tutsi army officers and about 50 000 Hutus and Tutsis were murdered in the violence this triggered.

In June 1992 the RPF and the Rwandan government accepted a cease-fire agreement at Arusha. A year later separate agreements on power-sharing in a 'Broad Based Transitional Government', the return of refugees, and the integration of armed forces were all signed, though tensions remained about their implementation. The United Nations Observer Mission Uganda–Rwanda (UNOMUR) was deployed in June 1993 on the Ugandan side of the Ugandan–Rwandan border to verify that no military assistance was entering Rwanda.

However, any hope that the two communities were moving towards accommodation was shattered by the events of the following year. Between April and June 1994 between 500 000 and 800 000 Tutsis and moderate Hutus were killed by Hutu militias in Rwanda. The genocide started when President

Habyarimana and his Burundian counterpart, Cyprien Ntar-yamira, were killed by unidentified assailants who fired at the presidential plane from an area under the control of Hutu forces. Immediately Tutsis and Hutu moderates were attacked by Hutu Interahamwe and Impuzamugambi militias, who were in possession of prepared death lists and who seemed to be acting in a co-ordinated manner. An interim extremist Hutu government was established in Kigali and, in retaliation, the Tutsi RPF resumed their military campaign on 8 April.

At the height of the genocide the daily killing rate was five times that of the Nazi death camps (Prunier, 1995: 261). Whereas in the Somali case the UN was criticized for strong-arm tactics in a delicate situation, in Rwanda its passivity as Hutu death squads carried out their genocide was an even greater blow to the image of the Organization. On 5 October 1993 Security Council Resolution 872 had established the United Nations Assistance Mission to Rwanda (UNAMIR). It had a mandate to contribute to the security of Kigali; monitor the cease-fire agreement; monitor the security situation leading up to elections; assist with mine clearance; investigate allegations of non-compliance with the Arusha Agreement; monitor the repatriation of refugees and the resettlement of displaced persons; assist in the co-ordination of humanitarian assistance; and investigate incidents regarding the activities of the gendarmerie and police.

When the genocide began, rather than reinforce this small UN force already in place, the UN actually evacuated most of its 2519 troops for their own protection after ten Belgian peacekeepers guarding the Prime Minister, Agathe Uwilin-giyimana, were killed and mutilated. So on 21 April the Security Council cut UNAMIR to 270 men and withdrew the rest, leaving their own Rwandan employees to an almost certain death. Melvern (1995: 13) recounts how Belgian peacekeepers, as they were flying out of Rwanda, slashed their blue berets because they were ashamed of what the UN was doing. The Secretariat did attempt to mobilize support to send a force of 5500 to the region after Security Council Resolution

912 on 21 April authorized the enlargement of UNAMIR, but this plan did not obtain US backing and the massacres in Rwanda continued without any effective international opposition. Resolution 918 of 17 May gave this force a mandate to help civilians, but since no Security Council member was willing to provide troops it lacked strength on the ground and so was an empty promise of protection.

The Belgian and French governments, however, were able to send small contingents to evacuate their own nationals and some members of the Hutu regime. The dispatch of a larger French force to Rwanda in June to create a 'safe zone' in a Hutu-controlled area made the UN inaction appear even more reprehensible. The Security Council conferred legitimacy on this 'Operation Turquoise' when Resolution 929 gave it a mandate under Chapter VII. However, its deployment was opposed by the RPF, though this seemed to soften once the force was in place. The French forces remained until August 1994, and then turned over the 'safe zone' to the newly established Rwandan Government of National Reconciliation. However, since many Hutus in this zone viewed this Tutsi-led government with suspicion the French withdrawal triggered a new mass exodus of refugees to Bukavu in Zaire.

The Hutu exodus from Rwanda had begun after the RPF took control of Kigali in June. Up to two million Hutus then fled into the refugee camps in Zaire, Uganda, Burundi and Tanzania. This new exodus put even greater pressure on humanitarian relief efforts. At the largest refugee camp at Goma, where over one million people were located, awful living conditions resulted in epidemics of cholera, dysentery and malaria that caused considerable loss of life. Prunier (1995: 303) estimates that 30 000 may have died there.

By August 1994, pitiably late, UNAMIR had increased its strength to over 3500 troops, with nearly all the main contingents coming from African states. It helped to train the new Rwandan police force, monitored the border with Zaire, and assisted with the rebuilding of the country's infrastructure. One of its other tasks was to protect the UN human rights monitors in Rwanda. This Human Rights Field Operation for Rwanda (HRFOR) was deployed after the genocide to monitor the human rights situation, facilitate the return of refugees and displaced persons, and investigate allegations of human rights abuses; but, sadly, it also failed to impress. It was poorly funded and some of its staff appeared to be badly prepared for the daunting task that they faced. Many were young and lacked the necessary linguistic skills. Prunier (1995: 343) notes that on 2 August 1994 the UN High Commissioner asked for 147 observers and by early September he was able to deploy just one, who had no budget, car or local staff. By November there were four observers. Manikas and Kumar (1997: 75), therefore, claim that 'from its inception, the UN's field operation in Rwanda was marred by conceptual confusion and an inadequate administrative capability . . . the field operation was saddled with a multifaceted mandate that was difficult to operationalize'.

The UN peacekeeping force was finally withdrawn in April 1996 amid a row with the government about who owned equipment left behind by the departing troops. Its impact on the genocide appeared to have been negligible. Prunier (1995: 275) makes the angry claim that the militiamen who carried out the genocide 'quickly understood that they had nothing to fear from these toy soldiers. The worst atrocities could be committed in their presence with total freedom from interference'.

Conclusion

In October 1995, the Organization's fiftieth birthday, a Special Assembly was convened in New York that was the largest gathering of world leaders in history. Yet all the glitz and ceremony could not hide the evidence of a chastened UN. That year a new Boutros-Ghali report entitled 'Supplement to an Agenda for Peace' highlighted certain problems that the

UN had encountered since 1992 and was notably less keen on the concept of peace-enforcement. The UN was also beset by financial worries and self-doubt about its own future. The *Independent* journalist David Usborne (1995) reported on the anniversary celebrations and noted that what was 'most striking about today's festivities may be the contrast between the idealism and excitement that surrounded the UN at its creation . . . and the aura of cynicism and exasperation that has settled about it today'. The fact that the UN had just established an Open Ended High Level Working Group to Consider the Revitalization and Strengthening of the UN System seemed to symbolize the sense of despondency.

By the end of 1995 I-FOR had replaced UNPROFOR in Bosnia. In Georgia attempts to establish an effective peace-keeping force came to nothing because of lack of resources and because Russia was opposed to a strong UN role in its 'near abroad'. Instead a small and ineffectual UN Observer Group in Georgia (UNOMIG) was created. The image of the UN as a weak organization was reinforced by the killing of more than 100 Lebanese civilians in an Israeli bombardment of the UN base at Qana in April 1996 and the unimpressive response to the problems in Zaire, where an inquiry into the massacres of Rwandan refugees could make no headway because it lacked the support of the new President Kabila.

Of course, it would be quite wrong to present an image of total failure in the mid-1990s. Humanitarian relief was delivered to the victims of conflict in both Bosnia and Somalia. In Macedonia UNPREDEP has taken the UN into the new and promising area of preventive peacekeeping. Peacekeeping missions did good work in places like Angola and Mozambique, though the peace process in the former is still bedevilled by the failure of UNITA to disarm. Here and elsewhere the Organization also assisted with the democratic transition that characterized the post-Cold War world.

The Bosnian and Somalian cases suggest that the UN is not well equipped to engage in peace-enforcement. Woods (1997: 167), who was a US official closely involved in the Somali case, claims that recent UN experience in Somalia, Bosnia and Rwanda indicates that:

> The UN is not up to such tasks and needs to be vastly improved and much more adequately financed if it is going to take on problems such as failed/failing states, genocide, and civil war or anarchy.

Large peacekeeping deployments also raise questions about their impact on local cultures and local economies. Their presence distorted the local economies in Somalia and Cambodia, and this has worried some peacekeeping analysts. Reports of human rights violations by some UN troops in Somalia added to a growing concern about the conduct of UN peacekeepers. Their involvement with prostitution and black-marketeering in Bosnia and Cambodia has also tarnished the image of peacekeeping. Simons (1995: 151–61) notes that in the Cambodian case there have even been accusations of UN personnel being involved in child prostitution.

The sense of disappointment with the UN was especially strong in the US. In mid-1996 Washington declared that it would veto the re-election of Boutros-Ghali for a second term. This occurred after clashes over a number of issues that included, for example, the release of a report about the Israeli shelling of the UN base in Qana, which killed over 100 Lebanese civilians. This challenged the Israeli claim that this had been an accident.

The Secretary-General turned down a private offer from the US that would have allowed him to serve for one more year before resigning, so unbending US opposition then meant that Boutros-Ghali had to stand down. He was replaced in 1997 by the experienced and popular UN Under Secretary-General, Kofi Annan. He was expected to lead an Organization reeling from some very public disasters, in severe financial crisis and perceived by some to be subservient to the US. Annan would have to make use of all his diplomatic skills to quiet the critics and improve the public image of the UN.

6

THE 'ADVANCEMENT OF ALL PEOPLES': THE UN AND WELFARE INTERNATIONALISM

We the people of the United Nations determined . . . to reaffirm our faith in fundamental human rights, in the dignity and worth of the human person, in the equal rights of men and women and of nations large and small . . . to promote social progress and better standards of life in larger freedom. (Preamble of the UN Charter)

No assessment of the contribution of the UN to international politics would be complete without a discussion of the Organization's work in the non-security realms. Because so much attention from the media and the academic community in the west has been directed at peace and security matters it is easy to forget that economic and social issues remain a vital concern for the majority of UN members. This is where most UN employees work and where most of the UN budget is spent. There is a plethora of specialized agencies and other UN bodies that have been working on an impressive range of economic, social and cultural issues throughout the world, organized into what Claude (1984: 68) has described as a 'kind of loose confederation'.

Claude goes on to claim that the UN represents a move away from 'the minimalist conception of the function of multilateral agencies to a kind of international New Dealism, an adaptation of the welfare state philosophy to the realm of world affairs' (Claude, 1984: 79). Armstrong, Lloyd and Redmond (1996: 66) agree with this assessment and claim that 'whereas the League's roots lay in the nineteenth century liberalism of the night-watchman state, the UN reflected the twentieth century liberalism of the welfare state'.

Welfare internationalism

Each specialized agency has a separate relationship with the United Nations, though most are modelled on the agreement between the UN and the International Labour Organization (ILO), which was the first such document to be negotiated. The ILO was established in 1919 and was the only League of Nations body to survive the Second World War. From its base in Geneva it attempts to promote fair and humane conditions of labour. Some of the other specialized agencies, such as the Food and Agriculture Organization (FAO), also pre-date the establishment of the six principal organs of the UN. Co-ordination between the Secretary-General and the specialized agencies is made more difficult because many of them do not even have their headquarters in New York.

Many of the weakest and most vulnerable victims of conflict and exploitation have had the quality of their lives improved by the work of bodies such as the United Nations Children's Emergency Fund (UNICEF), which in 1994 had programmes in 149 states (United Nations, 1997: 43). The United Nations High Commissioner for Refugees (UNHCR) has assisted millions of refugees and displaced persons. The United Nations Disaster Relief Co-ordinator (UNDRO), established in 1972, has helped to provide authoritative reports of relief needs and to co-ordinate relief efforts by UN agencies. The World Heath Organization (WHO) sets standards and guidelines for drugs and vaccines and has played a major role in the elimination of smallpox, which affected 15 million people in 1967. It is now playing an important part in the global battle against AIDS and in 1987 began a global programme to combat this disease. Experts working for WHO, which is based in Geneva, estimate that there will be between 30 and 40 million cases of HIV in men, women and children by the start of the twenty-first century (Whittaker, 1995: 263) The United Nations Educational, Scientific and Cultural Organization (UNESCO) has been fighting against illiteracy and contributes to the search for peace from its Paris headquarters through programmes for education and understanding. The World Food Programme (WFP) assisted 57 million poor and hungry people in 1994 (United Nations, 1997: 47).

In this brief study we cannot describe all of this work in detail. We have already mentioned some of the issues relating to development in previous chapters. So here we shall concentrate on the UN's work in two important areas, human rights and the protection of the environment. These are interesting areas because they reveal the extent of the divisions between the 'North' and 'South' on some key global issues. They seem to confirm the observation by Riddell-Dixon (1993: 1) that in the 1990s the 'dominant tension within the United Nations is between North and South – a development often conveniently overlooked by the North'.

Human rights

The League Covenant made no reference to individual human rights, but they are mentioned in the UN Charter in the preamble and articles 1, 53, 55, 56, 62 and 68. In the Assembly human rights issues are discussed in the third committee or in special committees established to examine, for example, Apartheid, Independence for Colonial Peoples or the Inalienable Rights of the Palestinian People to Self-determination. The

Assembly has also passed numerous non-binding declarations and resolutions on the elimination of discrimination against women, the rights of the child, torture, the elimination of all forms of intolerance and of discrimination based on religion or belief, the treatment of prisoners, and the rights of prisoners facing the death penalty.

The most important human rights body within the UN system is the Human Rights Commission (HRC), and its establishment in 1946 as a subsidiary body of ECOSOC (in accordance with Article 68 of the Charter) signalled 'the acceptance of human rights as a general part of the business of international society' (Vincent, 1986: 93). The HRC is now composed of 43 members who sit as representatives of governments. The Commission meets every year in February and March for six weeks, but its time is so limited that it rarely covers the whole of its agenda, which is packed with a wide range of items.

Alston (1992: 139) has noted that for 20 years the Commission insisted that it had 'no power to take any action in regard to any complaints concerning human rights'. However, in 1967 ECOSOC adopted Resolution 1253, which entitled the HRC to examine in public specific human rights violations by states. Many third world states hoped that this could be used to criticize racist and colonial governments, though it has also been used to publicize human rights abuses in other circumstances. Special Rapporteurs or experts have investigated cases in, for example, Afghanistan, Albania, Bolivia, Chile, Guatemala, Romania, Iraq, El Salvador, Cuba, Israeli Occupied Territories, Poland from 1982 to 1984, Equatorial Guinea and Haiti.

In 1970 ECOSOC Resolution 1503 gave the HRC and its Sub-Commission for the Prevention of Discrimination and the Protection of Minorities the right to examine in confidence communications which revealed a consistent pattern of gross human rights violations. This became known as the 1503 procedure. At least 45 states have been reported to the HRC under this practice (Alston 1992: 148). Even though this is a slow, secret mechanism open to political manipulation by states and blocs of states, it is, nonetheless, an important addition to the UN's human rights armoury. Nevertheless, it is important not to get carried away. Alston (1992: 173) comments that it is 'difficult to accept that, after almost half a century of concerted efforts, the principal UN procedures for responding to violations are quite as embryonic, marginally effective and unevenly applied as they are'.

The first major task of the HRC was to prepare the Universal Declaration of Human Rights, which was adopted by the General Assembly on 10 December 1948. It drew its inspiration from western texts on human rights and no state voted against it. However, Saudi Arabia, South Africa and the Soviet-bloc states abstained. The Declaration set out a number of basic rights such as the right to life, freedom of thought and conscience, the right to vote and the right to a fair trial. However, the Universal Declaration is not a legally binding document, and it took another 18 years for UN members to agree on how to give legal force to its principles. In the process, the initial idea of a single 'international Bill of Rights' gave way in 1951 to two International Covenants. Eventually, in January 1966, the UN agreed on the Covenant on Civil and Political Rights and the Covenant on Economic, Social and Cultural Rights. They are 'the most comprehensive statements of conventional human rights law yet adopted'(Hannum, 1995: 325). Both treaties came into force in 1976. The main reason why there were two covenants instead of one was that the superpower blocs could not agree on what to include in a single document. The western liberal democracies wanted to stress the classical liberal rights of the individual. The Marxist states wanted to stress group and class rights of a more economic and social nature.

The Covenant on Civil and Political Rights refers to the right to life and prohibits torture, inhuman and degrading treatment, and slavery. It also enshrines the right to a fair hearing, to freedom of thought, conscience and religion, and to freedom of expression and assembly. On the other hand the

Covenant on Economic, Social and Cultural Rights emphasizes the right to work and to just and favourable conditions at
work, the right to join a trade union, the right to social security
and the right to education. Mower (1985: 3) has argued that
economic and social rights are 'rights to certain opportunities
and conditions that are held to be essential if the individual is
to be able to enjoy what is commonly referred to as a decent
standard of living'. Both Covenants refer to the right of
national self-determination, a sign of the growing influence
of third world states at the UN.

A notable feature of the Covenant on Civil and Political
Rights was the establishment of a Human Rights Committee,
not to be confused with the Human Rights Commission. The
committee is composed of 18 members chosen from states that
have ratified the Covenant. Unlike the HRC representatives,
these members are meant to serve in a personal capacity and
are not meant to act as government delegates. This committee
scrutinizes reports from states on how they have incorporated
the Covenant into their own law. However, it tends to be
rather cautious and it does not refer to any individual cases of
human rights abuse. Also, there is no real incentive for states to
take their responsibilities seriously and co-operation by states is
entirely voluntary. Their representatives are not obliged to
answer questions and the committee has no choice but to
accept the answers given to it. Thus, although the committee
may ask for additional information, 'states actually provide
only what they choose' (Donnelly, 1994: 207). However, states
can sign an optional protocol which gives the committee the
right to hear petitions from individuals in these states. Only
about one-third of all states have signed this. Although the
final decisions of the committee are made public, considerations of complaints from individuals take place in secret and
the records of the committee's discussions are confidential.

In 1985 a Committee on Economic, Social and Cultural
Rights was established as an independent expert committee.
This followed several unsuccessful attempts by a working
group to create an effective supervisory body for the 1966

Covenant on Economic, Social and Cultural Rights as part of ECOSOC's own machinery. The US was opposed to this committee, and has retained a consistent dislike of the whole idea of economic and social rights. Unlike the Human Rights Committee, the Committee on Economic, Social and Cultural Rights has no mandate deriving from the 1966 Covenants, since it is not mentioned there. However, in many other respects it works like the Human Rights Committee.

The UN is now trying to develop a 'third generation' of rights, such as the right to development, the right to peace, and the right to a clean environment. In 1979 the Assembly agreed that every nation and every human being has 'the inherent right to life in peace'. In 1986 it adopted the Declaration on the Right to Development, with only the US voting against. These 'peoples' rights' tend to be supported most fervently by third world states, especially in Africa. In 1981, for example, the Organization of African Unity adopted the Banjul Charter on Human and Peoples' Rights. Peoples' rights include the right to exploit natural resources, the right to a life free from foreign domination, and the right to development (see Ferguson, 1986; Okoth-Ogenda, 1993).

At the same time as the General Assembly adopted the Universal Declaration it also agreed the International Convention on the Prevention and Punishment of the Crime of Genocide. This made it an offence to undertake actions with the intent to destroy in whole or in part a national, ethnic, racial or linguistic group. A number of acts were also identified as constituting genocide: killing members of a group; causing serious bodily or mental harm; deliberately inflicting conditions of life calculated to result in the physical destruction of the group; actions to prevent births within the group; and the transfer of children out of the group. Sadly, however, until recently the UN has been reluctant to invoke this Convention. This has led to some caustic criticisms of the UN, most notably by Kuper (1985). The reluctance to respond to genocide can be seen as a symptom of a more general indisposition to deal with the protection of ethnic minorities (Ryan, 1990).

After adopting the two 1966 Covenants the UN convened a major human rights conference at Tehran in 1968. Over 80 states attended and although they all voted that the 1948 Universal Declaration constituted an obligation for members of the international community, serious disagreements emerged between the North and the South. Third world states wanted to give much more prominence to racism, colonialism and self-determination and were intent on criticising South Africa and Israel. Many western governments wanted to focus on other human rights issues.

After Tehran the UN continued to expand its human rights remit. Discrimination against women received major attention. A Commission on the Status of Women had been created by ECOSOC in 1946, and this body worked on a number of issues relating to its mandate, which is to prepare recommendations and reports on 'promoting women's rights in political, economic, civil, social and educational fields'. A major step forward occurred in 1975, when the first international conference on women to be sponsored by the UN convened in Mexico City. The 8000 delegates adopted the Mexico Declaration on Equality of Women and their Contribution to Development and Peace. The following year the Assembly adopted a Declaration on the Elimination of Discrimination Against Women and began work on the Convention Against All Forms of Discrimination Against Women. This was adopted by the Assembly on 18 December 1979 and came into force in 1981 (United Nations, 1993b). The Convention recognizes that extensive discrimination against women still exists and commits signatories to take all appropriate measures to eliminate this discrimination in the fields of education, employment, health care, the law, and marriage and family relations. Article 17 created a Committee on the Elimination of Discrimination against Women to consider reports from states on how they are implementing the provisions of the convention.

Other UN conventions worthy of note include the 1969 Convention on the Elimination of all Forms of Racial Discrimination (CERD) and the 1989 Convention on the Rights of the Child. Article 9 of CERD requires states to submit periodic reports to the UN Committee on the Elimination of Racial Discrimination and the Convention on the Rights of the Child has established a monitoring body called the Committee on the Rights of the Child that also examines reports by states that have ratified the convention.

Tensions in the human rights system re-emerged at the huge World Conference on Human Rights held in Vienna in the middle of 1993. Five thousand delegates from about 170 states met to debate the UN's human rights role, though no analysis of individual cases of human rights abuses was allowed. Nonetheless there were squabbles between India and Pakistan over Kashmir, between Portugal and Indonesia about East Timor and between Israel and Palestine. A major fault line emerged between the developed west and several third world states. These divisions had always been present in one form or another. In the 1980s, for example, Iran had criticized the two 1966 covenants because they were not fully consistent with Islamic doctrines (Quinn, 1992: 71). Now the divisions seemed wider than ever. Some Asian states such as China, Indonesia and Malaysia were wary of emphasizing universal rights because they feared that this could be characterized as a western attempt to impose alien values on their cultures. This argument was reflected in the 1993 Bangkok Declaration, where Asian and Pacific states claimed that human rights declarations should take account of national and regional particularities and different cultures and backgrounds.

At Vienna, however, the US led the resistance to such relativistic arguments and pushed strongly for a reaffirmation of universal rights. Thus the final document accepted that states had a solemn commitment to promote universal respect for human rights and fundamental freedoms and that the promotion and protection of human rights was a legitimate concern of the international community. A measure of relativism did appear in the final document in Section 1: 5 of the Vienna Declaration and Programme of Action. This states that 'the significance of national and regional particularities and various historical, cultural and religious backgrounds must be borne in mind'. But the main thrust of the Declaration was to restate and defend the concept of universal rights. So the very first paragraph argues that the universal nature of human rights and fundamental freedoms is 'beyond question'.

Many states also wanted the human rights agenda to give a much more prominent place to 'third generation' rights. One recalls here the comment of René Cassin that 'the right to life, that's not only the right not to be condemned to death by arbitrary power or the right not to be murdered – it's also the right to eat!' (Best, 1983: 10). Some progress was made here and the 1986 General Assembly Declaration that development was a universal and an unalienable right and an integral part of fundamental human rights was unanimously affirmed at Vienna.

The idea of a High Commissioner for Human Rights was also discussed at Vienna. This was a proposal with a 'long history' (Humphrey, 1984: 296–301) and although no agreement could be reached at Vienna the General Assembly was asked to consider this issue as a matter of priority. The post was approved by the General Assembly in Resolution 48/141 on 20 December 1993 and José Ayala Lasso of Equador was appointed the first High Commissioner with a mandate to promote and protect the effective enjoyment of all human rights and to co-ordinate the promotion and protection of these rights throughout the UN system. He tried to keep human rights issues on the international agenda through visits and his inputs at international gatherings. Lasso was also given the responsibility of co-ordinating the implementation of the UN Decade for Human Rights Education. The UN Secretary-General appeared to be opposed to this new post before it was created by the Assembly, but it had the strong support of the US and of many impartial observers who thought that the new office could raise the profile of human rights within the UN system. Despite these developments it is difficult to be too enthusiastic about the Vienna Conference. As one observer noted:

> While the World Conference did not collapse and managed to produce a final document with no apparent dissenters, it did not produce any new breakthroughs and it failed to confront many of the UN's shortcomings in promoting and protecting human rights. (Matthews, 1993: 34)

Another interesting development in the human rights field is the inclusion of human rights tasks in UN peacekeeping missions. Here special reference can be made to the UN mission to El Salvador (ONUSAL). This was the first peace-keeping operation to include human rights observers (about 120), who were mandated to engage in human rights monitoring through a network of regional and sub-regional offices throughout this central American state. However, this mission was criticized for being too timid because it seemed to be reluctant to criticize the government of El Salvador (Simons, 1994: 186).

Also worthy of note are the two *ad hoc* tribunals set up to investigate and prosecute war crimes in Rwanda and the former Yugoslavia. All the permanent members of the Security Council are suspicious of attempts to establish a more permanent institution to prosecute war criminals, but the US and France have expressed the most vocal opposition to a strong and independent International Criminal Court that could implement a more consistent response to breaches of the laws of war and the Genocide Convention.

The International Criminal Tribunal for the former Yugoslavia (ICTFY) was established by Security Council Resolution 827 on 27 May 1993. It is authorized to investigate events in the former Yugoslavia since 1991 and has the power to prosecute suspects, though its jurisdiction has been rejected by Bosnian Serbs. After several years most war criminals remain unpunished, though there have been some arrests of those indicted at the Hague. In July 1997, for example, British soldiers attached to S-FOR arrested one Bosnian Serb and killed another in one such arrest operation. Yet many of those indicted remain at large including 'big fish' such as Bosnian Serb leaders Radovan Karadzic and Ratko Mladic.

In the Rwandan case the international tribunal, based in Arusha in northern Tanzania and Kigale in Rwanda, was established after a commission of experts created by the Security Council decided months after the killings had started that genocide had been committed in Rwanda. However it has faced many difficulties. Many prosecution lawyers are young and inexperienced. There have been allegations of misconduct by some key officials at the tribunal and some African states have been reluctant to co-operate. A lack of funding has created difficulties and disagreements have also arisen between the *ad hoc* tribunal and the government of Rwanda, which wants its own system for trying those accused of war crimes to have precedence over the UN body. The Rwandan government criticized a Security Council Resolution that prohibited the *ad hoc* tribunal from awarding the death penalty and thought that it should have been based in Kigali so that all Rwandans could have access to the proceedings. Whereas the UN tribunal has indicted only a few dozen suspected war criminals the Rwandan authorities are holding up to 90 000 suspects in gaol.

There is a clear strain between the UN's role in easing interstate diplomacy and its role in promoting an agenda based on international welfare and social justice. Member governments often give the impression that the promotion of human rights gets in the way of 'normal' interstate activity. Why, for example, criticize China for its human rights record in Tibet if this will put at risk political and economic relations with Beijing? Outside UN meetings, where official representatives pay lip-service to high standards of behaviour, many states show little interest in human rights issues, especially if turning a blind eye benefits their own national interest. For example, Maurice Abrams (1979), a US representative on the Human Rights Commission between 1965 and 1968, states that he was instructed by Washington not to condemn the human rights record of US allies such as Greece and Haiti during his period of service. Even when states do take up human rights issues partiality means there is always a danger that the debate becomes a 'sinister farce' (Hoffmann, 1981: 117).

Nothing illustrates this more forcefully than the treatment of the Dutch Director of the UN's own Human Rights Division, Theo van Boven. He upset senior UN figures and some influential governments by his robust criticism of regimes guilty of serious human rights abuses. They were accustomed to bland and innocuous statements on human rights issues, but at the start of the 1982 Human Rights Commission meetings van Boven singled out seven governments for attack, including El Salvador and Guatemala. This not only upset many Latin American authoritarian regimes, but also infuriated the Reagan administration in the US, which supported these governments and was trying to argue that their human rights records were improving. The US government was already suspicious of van Boven because he had attended a human rights conference organized by the Sandinista administration in Nicaragua. The Dutchman's approach also upset Moscow, which did not want UN officials taking such a strong line against human rights abuses. So van Boven was removed from his post when his contract was not renewed by Secretary-General de Cuellar.

Human rights concerns are often downplayed when they clash with the interests of states. Hence the UN found itself unable to take a strong stand against major human rights abusers such as Pol Pot in Cambodia or Idi Amin in Uganda. Successive Secretaries-General have also tended to relegate human rights issues at the UN because they endangered the political work of the Secretariat in other areas. Hoffmann (1981: 116) explains that states have a diverse range of important concerns. However:

If one starts denouncing countries whose support one needs in all of those arenas, where will one be? But if one tries to balance off each of these concerns against human rights, what kind of crazy quilt will one get?

It may be that the UN does not yet have the balance right. Although Secretaries-General have taken up human rights issues in public and private, the UN tends to give priority to 'peace' rather than 'justice' (Ramcharan, 1987: 159).

The environment

Unlike human rights, there is no mention of the environment in the UN Charter. Indeed, it was not until the 1970s that environmentalism became an important issue at the United Nations. As public unease rose about nuclear testing, the use of insecticides such as DDT, and the pollution of air, land and sea, a conference on the environment was convened in Stockholm from 5 to 16 June 1972. Although most Soviet-bloc states did not attend because of a dispute over whether the German Democratic Republic should be accorded a status equal to West Germany, 114 states and 200 non-governmental organizations participated in what one analyst called 'the landmark event in the growth of international environmentalism' (McCormick, 1989: 88).

Several important initiatives did, indeed, emerge from this gathering. The United Nations Environmental Programme (UNEP) was established in Nairobi by the General Assembly in December 1972. A Declaration on the Human Environment, made up of 26 principles, was agreed after protracted negotiation, and 109 recommendations were included in a Plan of Action. The years from 1972 to 1982 were declared a decade for solving environmental problems.

However, certain doubts were also raised by poor states who feared that environmentalism, which they regarded as a rich state's disease, would restrict their economic growth, increase the cost of development and raise prices for their products in international markets. One of the Chinese delegation, for example, argued that 'each country has the right to determine its own environmental standards and policies in the light of its own conditions, and no country whatsoever should undermine the interests of the developing countries under the pretext of protecting the environment' (McCormick, 1989: 99). Although there may indeed be only one planet earth, it seems that there are a number of different views about how we should treat it.

UNEP, under its first director Maurice Strong, initiated a series of programmes that attempted to monitor the global environment and educate people about the dangers of its degradation and pollution. An 'earthwatch' network was established to monitor environmental conditions. In 1974 it also began a Regional Seas Programme that has addressed pollution in places like the Mediterranean, the Red Sea, the Persian Gulf and the Caribbean. Other issues tackled include desertification, deforestation, and the management of hazardous waste.

In June 1982 there was a major conference involving 105 states in Nairobi. It reaffirmed many of the principles endorsed at Stockholm. Yet again there were complaints voiced by the poorer states who wanted to place development above the environment. In 1987 the World Commission on Environment and Development (1987), also called the Brundtland Commission after its chairperson, issued its influential report. The commission had been created by the General Assembly and it attempted to reconcile the competing demands of 'environmentalists' and 'developmentalists' with the concept of sustainable development. It called for economic growth to be stimulated, claiming that poverty is a major source of environmental degradation; but also recommended that environmental resources should be preserved. This approach, which seemed to ignore significant differences of opinion between the two camps, was endorsed by the UNEP and by the World Bank. The same year a UNEP conference adopted the Montreal Protocol on Substances that Deplete the Ozone Layer. Indeed, in the 1980s atmospheric pollution emerged as one of the key environmental issues.

One manifestation of this concern was the creation of the International Panel on Climate Change in November 1988. This was made up of scientific experts who were to investigate the factors affecting climate change and to forecast and assess trends. In 1990 it produced a report that predicted that environmental damage, leading to changes in climate, would have a devastating effect on the lives of millions with a significant increase in desertification, agricultural disruption and shoreline erosion. The work of this International Panel, along with the Brundtland Report, played an important role in setting the agenda for the next major global environmental conference.

The 1992 United Nations Conference on the Environment and Development (UNCED) retained the link between environmental and development issues. This 'Earth Summit', convened in Rio de Janeiro, was the largest conference ever held up to this date. Over 3500 delegates attended and over 100 heads of state addressed the gathering. A number of initiatives emerged. The Earth Charter was a rather bland statement. The non-binding Agenda 21, signed by 178 states, was lengthier and was intended to be a blueprint for action. It called for an increase in growth, a reduction in poverty, a decline in population pressure, fairer use of the global commons, a reduction in the generation of waste and an increased centrality for environmental and development issues.

A Convention on Biological Diversity, which sought to preserve plant and animal species, was adopted by 140 states. A Convention on Climate Change, also known as the Framework Convention, obtained 155 signatories. This focused on 'greenhouse gases' in the atmosphere and declared that emission levels would be held at 1990 levels until the year 2000. This was not a significant reduction because the US government, urged on by American businesses opposed to environmental regulation, insisted that more stringent controls were unacceptable. The UN's own independent Inter-governmental Panel on Climate Change challenged the low targets agreed at Rio in a major report in 1994. It doubted if stabilizing emissions at 1990 levels would be enough to protect the atmosphere and predicted that further drastic action would be required.

A proposed convention on deforestation had to be abandoned when no consensus could be reached between northern and southern states. Instead a non-binding Declaration on Forest Principles was agreed. Finally, a new environmental body emerged as a result of the ruminations at Rio. In 1993 ECOSOC established a United Nations Commission on Sustainable Development based in New York. It is to monitor the implementation of the Rio agreements and serve as a forum for developing policies for sustainable development.

Limitations

Since the end of the Cold War more opportunities have arisen to raise both human rights and environmental issues at the global level. The growing significance of human rights issues at the UN can be seen in the debates about humanitarian intervention and the calls to apply the full force of international law to those guilty of genocide in Rwanda and Bosnia. Green issues are also now a significant component of the international agenda and the fear of environmental destruction is prompting a redefinition of security to include the protection of nature. Vogler (1997: 243) notes that summit meetings between the leaders of the G7 'now make declarations about forests and pollution alongside their more traditional preoccupations with interest rates and "political" and security issues'.

Yet although both human rights and environmental issues are eroding the traditional distinction between 'high' and 'low' politics, that is, the distinction between security and welfare issues, we should not overstate their impact on interstate relations or claim that they are of central importance even at the UN. We can feel the sense of disappointment in the analysis of many commentators in assessing the achievements in these two areas.

Amnesty International (1992), for example, points out that:

> the UN still has difficulty in confronting pressing human rights issues directly or taking effective action in response to urgent situations of gross violations, particularly when dealing with unresponsive or uncooperative governments.

Imber (1996: 150), assessing the contributions of the UN to the protection of the environment, concludes that although the UN is the best place to conduct environmental diplomacy because it is the most important global forum for creating new norms, it is also the worst place, because it is just an organization of states and excludes many key actors.

We should note that work in these areas is not properly resourced. Both the UN Centre for Human Rights and the UNEP have suffered from lack of funding, which has led to understaffing. The secretariats of both UN bodies are located away from New York, with the Centre for Human Rights based in Geneva and UNEP in Nairobi. Such arrangements make co-ordination between the Secretary-General and the specialized agencies more difficult and may reduce the influence of such agencies on UN policy. As the human rights agenda is becoming more significant, the geographic distance between the UN's political centre and its main human rights organ is becoming less defensible (van Boven, 1992: 578). Either the Centre for Human Rights should be moved to New York or its liaison office there should be upgraded. Furthermore, although the UN has set standards it lacks an effective independent monitoring system and fact-finding capability. Nor can it enforce these standards.

It is also important to note that great powers continue to shape the agenda for these issues. At Rio in 1992 the US opposed strict controls on the environment and so certain proposals had to be watered down. At Vienna the following year the US supported the idea of a High Commissioner for Human Rights, and such a post was created. This reminds us that the closing gap between high and low politics works both ways. It forces the great powers to take heed of economic and social issues, but it also thrusts the agendas of these powers into discussions of such matters.

Global summits

The trend towards large, high-profile 'world conferences' or 'summits' is seen in other areas of the UN's social agenda. In 1994 there was the Cairo Conference on population and development. This adopted a plan of action to enable states to make reproductive health and family planning available to all by 2015 and reaffirmed that any form of coercion for family planning is unacceptable.

In March 1995 the World Summit on Social Development was held in Copenhagen. This issued a declaration aimed at reducing unemployment and poverty and focused on some of the negative aspects of globalization. In September the same year the UN Fourth World Conference on Women adopted the 'Global Platform for Action'. This was endorsed by all 189 delegations and identifies critical areas of concern and is supposed to promote equality for women. It suggests a number of 'strategic actions' in areas such as poverty, education, health care, violence, employment, the portrayal of women in the media and the role of women in decision-making.

The question has sometimes been asked whether anything positive emerges from these international media events. Critics argue that these large UN conferences attract heads of government who see them only as photo opportunities and who offer no leadership or vision for the serious issues under discussion. Accusations of hypocrisy are, therefore, easy to make. Such meetings certainly bring to public attention the tensions that still exist between different states about social issues and all too frequently the fine words agreed at these meetings are never translated into political practice and few resources are made available to implement well-meaning plans. They therefore can illustrate, ironically, that the UN is a rather powerless body.

However such meetings help to institutionalize the notion of international responsibility and establish forums for non-governmental organizations (Forsyth, 1995). Fomerand (1996) also supports such events and argues that they serve three important functions: the creation, dissemination and sharing of knowledge; monitoring and early warning; and standard setting. He also emphasizes the opportunities these gatherings present for greater NGO involvement in these issues. They can therefore be viewed as part of a process of the social mobilization that is accompanying 'globalization'.

Article 71 of the Charter allows ECOSOC to 'make suitable arrangements for consultation with non-governmental organizations which are concerned with matters within its competence'. Such arrangements often involve placing NGOs into one of two categories. Category 1 NGOs are those that can claim to represent major segments of the population in a large number of countries. They can propose agenda items and may, on occasions, make oral interventions during ECOSOC meetings. Category II NGOs, like those in the first category, can send observers to ECOSOC meetings and submit written statements. They have an international reputation and a special competence in the areas covered by ECOSOC. One analysis of the growing importance of NGOs in the UN system has found that 92 UN agencies now have NGO liaison offices in many parts of the world (Alger, 1994: 308). Over 840 NGOs attended the Vienna Human Rights Conference, whilst at the Rio Earth Summit the NGOs convened a Global Forum to run parallel with the official meetings.

However, such gatherings also demonstrate that there is an absence of consensus on some key items. Tensions between the representatives of secular liberal states and those subject to Islamic or Catholic influences were obvious at the 1995 Women's Conference in Beijing over issues such as access to contraception and equal status. Many third world states remain suspicious of the western emphasis on environmentalism, and are worried that the human rights issue could be used to legitimize intervention in their internal affairs. Therefore, as the UN becomes more active in social and cultural areas major disagreements can emerge about the significance to be given to cultural distinctiveness and to differences between rich and poor states. UN responses to issues such as human rights and environmental protection have often been inspired by western values. Perhaps Galtung (1994) is correct to call for a more balanced normative input into these global debates.

CONCLUSION: NEW HORIZONS AND OLD RESTRICTIONS

We have created unprecedented possibilities for both progress and disaster on our planet without yet assuming the collective responsibility that both these possibilities demand. We already have much of the machinery for this purpose. We must take it out, overhaul it, and get it on the road. (Urquhart, 1987: 378)

In the course of this study we have identified a number of tensions and contradictions at the heart of the UN. It is an organization wedded firmly to the state-centric view of international politics on a planet that is becoming more interdependent and 'globalized'. It is also committed to respect the sovereignty of its members in a world where there is a 'disappearing boundary between internal and international conflicts' (Rupesinghe: 1992).

Many of the most destructive conflicts today are 'internal', where one or more of the actors are not states but ethnic groups. The humanitarian problems such conflicts cause can be spotlighted immediately by journalists with satellite up-links. They are also likely to spill over to become regional problems and can therefore take on an interstate dimension. This may be because they threaten regional security, trigger acts of international terrorism, violate international standards of human rights, or they create significant refugee flows (Ryan, 1995). Yet many members still feel uncomfortable with authorizing action in situations which still fall mainly within the internal affairs of states. So the UN has played no significant role in the conflicts in most of the successor states of the USSR, in India, in Sri Lanka, Sudan, Tibet, Kurdish areas of Turkey, Burma and Peru.

The UN is a meeting place, a catalyst for co-operation and dialogue that can be used to improve co-ordination between states. Yet it can also be an arena, used by governments as just another battleground in their struggles with each other. Any analysis of the work of the Organization during the Cold War, for example, has to concede that it was used as a propaganda weapon by both superpowers, but that these superpowers also found it useful to call on its services in volatile areas such as the Middle East.

Other tensions can also be pointed out. The UN is meant to be an international organization but remains perilously dependent on the US for money and other resources. In the face of the ambivalent attitude of the US to the UN, and the perpetual tensions between the White House and Congress over policy, some believe that the UN should reduce its dependence on Washington. The influential Independent Commission on Disarmament and Security Issues (1982), also known as the Palme Report, suggested that no state should have to pay more than 15 per cent of assessed contributions, though even this reduced figure may be too high.

The UN is also supposed to operate on the basis of the equality of states. Article 2 (1) of the Charter states that the 'Organization is based on the principle of the sovereign equality of all its members'. Yet there is clearly a hierarchy at the UN, with the five permanent members of the Security Council having a special status that gives them the right to veto any UN action that they find objectionable.

The UN's contribution to international peace and security

Nicholas (1959) argues that when it comes to promoting international peace and security there are a number of techniques that the UN can employ, usually in combination. They are: investigation and fact-finding (for example, Greek frontier incidents), interposition and monitoring through peacekeeping and observer missions, conciliation and good offices, recommendation (for example, Security Council Resolution 242 on the Middle East) and appeal. Akashi (1995–6) points out that the UN can still make important contributions at all stages of the conflict cycle: prevention, assistance to victims of violence, crisis management, mediation, and post-conflict peacebuilding.

The UN, especially the General Assembly, acts as an international forum for states. Of course lengthy speech-making and political posturing can be tedious and uninspiring. It is certainly true that in public there is a tendency for meetings to adopt a parliamentary style, with different groups trying to outvote each other. This is what Morgenthau (1967: 535) termed the 'vice of majority decision'.

Yet such debates allow all states to set out their views on international issues and therefore they serve as a mechanism whereby governments can be educated about each other's attitudes and intentions. States are then more able to understand international opinion about specific issues. It also allows states to bring issues to the attention of the international community without having to resort to violence. Diplomatic contacts are eased, issues can be defined and agendas are set through what Claude (1984: 336) has called the 'grand debate'. In this way the UN has contributed to peaceful change through interstate co-operation and eased violent confrontation, contributing to international peace and security through collective legitimization (through resolutions and conventions) and collective delegitimization (for example, colonialism and apartheid). Public debates should not always, therefore, be dismissed as meaningless since they allow states or blocs of states to express their views on matters that are important to them. Issues such as racism and apartheid, colonialism and development became much more visible because of debates at the UN.

However, a great deal of the most effective work of the UN does not take place in the open. The extensive diplomatic presence at UN headquarters facilitates direct face-to-face contact out of the public glare. Several commentators have emphasized this role of the UN. O'Brien (1968: 247) pointed out that the UN 'provides opportunities for continuous contact, and unpublicized adjustments of matters in dispute. Indeed states which are publicly inveighing against each other on the floor of the Assembly may at the same time be working out a compromise behind the scenes.' Goodwin (1957: 211) agreed and claimed that 'the real business of the United Nations is now conducted in relative privacy outside the formal meetings'. These opportunities for diplomatic contact benefit all states, but are especially valuable for poorer members of the UN, who cannot afford to have extensive diplomatic relations with all other states individually.

The Organization also has a significant role to play in developing international law. This occurs in several ways (Schachter and Joyner, 1995). The International Law Commission (ILC), created by the Assembly in 1947, has helped to codify law by changing customary law into treaty law. Examples here include work done on the law of the sea and diplomatic relations. The UN has also produced conventions on a wide range of human rights issues, some of which were discussed in Chapter 6. The ICJ, through its judicial decisions, has also helped to clarify and interpret law. It can also be used to provide legally binding decisions in certain disputes, though its significance has been affected by the unwillingness of states to accept its jurisdiction in cases that involve their vital interests.

The UN and its specialized agencies have also helped develop international regimes in areas such as the protection of human rights, the control of weapons of mass destruction, the promotion of development, and humanitarian assistance for the victims of man-made and natural disasters. More recently it has increased its efforts in the fight against AIDS and the control of illicit drug-trafficking.

The Secretary-General can also command a certain amount of moral authority, since he upholds the principles of the Charter that have been accepted by all member states and can represent the views of the 'international community'. He can therefore be a credible and effective third party. In addition, because the Secretary-General is usually picked from a small neutral or non-aligned state he is less likely to be seen as an agent of one or other power block.

It is vital that the Secretary-General does not lose the confidence of any of the major powers. Yet the record suggests that this is no easy task. Both Lie and Hammarskjøld failed to maintain support from the USSR. Waldheim's re-election to a third term was stopped by China, and the US, against the wishes of the vast majority of UN members, forced Boutros-Ghali to stand down as Secretary-General at the end of 1996. It was a fear of antagonizing one or other superpower that induced a cautious approach from most Secretaries-General, though this was most noticeable in the U Thant, Waldheim and de Cuellar eras.

Despite these constraints the Secretary-General has been able to engage in direct diplomacy or has appointed special representatives to serve as mediators or conciliators. Ellsworth Bunker contributed to the negotiations that led to the agreement between the Netherlands and Indonesia over West Irian. Luis Weckmann-Munoz helped Iran and Iraq to reach a temporary agreement about their border dispute in 1974, whilst Nils Gussing helped to reduce tensions between Thailand and Cambodia in the 1950s (Puchala, 1993). Diego Cordovez played an important role in the 'proximity talks' that led to the 1988 Geneva Accords which allowed the USSR to withdraw from Afghanistan, and successive Special Representatives have also struggled to maintain momentum in the intercommunal talks in Cyprus since 1968. Cyrus Vance was able to arrange a cease-fire between the Croatian government and Croatian Serbs in 1992 and paved the way for the deployment of UNPROFOR.

By using peacekeeping forces the UN helped to stabilize and contain conflicts that could otherwise have spread throughout a particular region. Some have complained that this leads to no more than a 'controlled impasse', but even this is an achievement where a cease-fire may not be self-sustaining. The blue helmets have been used to manage and limit violence in many bitter conflicts, and they are increasingly being used to contribute to post-conflict reconstruction through election monitoring, human rights monitoring, and the training of civilian police.

Events in Bosnia and Somalia have revealed some of the problems that can arise when the UN moves beyond traditional peacekeeping operations into the area of peace-enforcement. For the UN lacks the military capability, unity of purpose and the organizational cohesion to undertake such action, which also threatens to undermine the impartiality of the organization and to confuse the mandates of peacekeeping operations. UN peacekeeping and peace-enforcement operations peaked in 1994 and 1995 and the number of troops on UN service has dropped considerably since then. Collective Security through military action clearly has not worked except when the US has been willing to take a strong role in the enforcement of peace and there has not been serious opposition from other permanent members of the Security Council.

The UN will, therefore, re-establish the distinction between peacekeeping and peace-enforcement which were, in the words of Falk (1996: 96), 'imprudently merged'. This does not mean that the UN will never engage again in peace-enforcement under Chapter VII, but influential member states are now extremely wary of this role and the UN itself feels more comfortable with its traditional peacekeeping function under Chapter VI. In the near future use of Chapter VII seems likely to be confined to the implementation of economic sanctions

(Iraq, Serbia, Libya) or arms embargoes (Rwanda and Haiti). Many third world states, fearful of a decline in respect for state sovereignty, will welcome this return to a less interventionist organization.

Improvements to traditional peacekeeping can be made. Missions need better training and preparation (United States Institute of Peace, 1994); more efficient management; pre-stocking of equipment; and a harmonization of standards, communications and command and control. The creation of a 'lessons-learned unit' in the Department of Peacekeeping in 1995 may also help to strengthen the institutional memory of the organization. We could also see UN peacekeepers move into new areas such as drug interdiction and naval and airforce peacekeeping.

It might also be possible to improve the reaction to crises by creating a new early-warning centre linked to an effective global monitoring system (International Alert, 1993). Of course this would be next to useless if there is not also a capacity for rapid reaction to crises, so several commentators have called on the UN to develop a way of responding more effectively and quickly to crises, pointing out that 'the UN's capacity for rapid and effective action before a situation gets completely out of hand is virtually non-existent' (Urquhart, 1995: 3). This could be done through stand-by forces allocated to the UN by member states, or by a rapid reaction force comprised of a corps of UN volunteers with previous peace-keeping experience. This is not a new idea, but it has received more attention in recent years. In 1993, for example, the UN established a Stand-by Forces Planning Team and a year later created a Stand-by Arrangement System where states were able to express a willingness to supply certain units for UN missions. However, states still have to approve individual deployments. Quick responses to crises also require financial resources, and a reserve fund to cover the initial costs of an operation would be useful here.

One should also note the British government's idea of 'wider peacekeeping' (Ministry of Defence: 1995). This was an attempt to define what UN personnel should, and should not, do on operations where they do not have the consent of all of the parties, especially at the 'tactical', grass-roots level. Though it was important to preserve consent at the strategic level, at the tactical level the edge of consent is unclear. One of the key ideas here is that UN peacekeepers do not have to obtain the consent of the parties for everything that they do at this level, as long as they retain general support and as long as the use of force is proportional, has specific ends, and is the last resort. Peacekeepers may, therefore, be able to take much more robust action in certain circumstances without affecting their general credibility and reputation for impartiality.

We are also likely to see greater co-operation with regional and sub-regional organizations, which have increased their role in the area of peacekeeping, sometimes in partnership with the UN. Examples here include the work of ECOMOG and the UN in Liberia, the UN and the OAS in Haiti, the UN and the Commonwealth of Independent States in Georgia, and the UN and NATO in the former Yugoslavia. It is not surprising, therefore, that in 1994 General Assembly Declaration 49/57 calls for the 'Enhancement of Co-operation Between the United Nations and Regional Arrangements or Agencies in the Maintenance of International Peace and Security'.

The resurgence of regionalism since the end of the Cold War means that there now exists a wide range of effective regional bodies that the UN could work with (Hurrell, 1995). This would move the UN from Chapters VI and VII of the Charter to Chapter VIII, which deals with 'regional arrangements'. Article 53 states that the Security Council 'shall, where appropriate, utilize such regional arrangements or agencies for enforcement action under its authority'. So we will probably see more use made of what Boutros-Ghali called the 'new division of labour between the United Nations and Regional Organizations' (Weiss, 1995a: 180), or what Franck (1995) has termed the 'franchise model' of international peace and security. However, there have been clear deficiencies with regional peacekeeping in the past and the experience of UN–NATO relations in Bosnia demonstrates how difficult operations involving more than one international agency can be. Despite the problems in Bosnia, however, NATO abides by a North Atlantic Council decision of December 1992 to offer support to UN peacekeeping operations.

The UN has also proved itself useful in offering parties to a conflict a 'face-saving' device, allowing them to make concessions to the Organization rather than the enemy. Examples include the UK and France during the 1956 Suez crisis, the Netherlands over the future of West Irian in 1962, and the Soviet Union in Afghanistan.

It is difficult to quantify the contribution of the UN to international peace and security. During the Cold War period statistical analyses were not encouraging for the UN. Northedge and Donelan (1971) analysed 50 international disputes between 1945 and 1970 and found that there was extensive UN involvement in 17 cases, minimal UN involvement in 25 cases and no involvement in eight cases. They concluded that the UN's record 'both in resolving international disputes by agreement and in helping them become quiescent is by no means impressive' (Northedge and Donelan, 1971: 239). Beer (1981: 100) refers to studies which suggest that of 31 two-party conflicts submitted to the UN between 1945 and 1966, 81 per cent were unresolved or were settled outside the Organization. Riggs and Plano (1994: 154) argue that the UN's record of peaceful settlement is 'statistically not strong'. They quote the work of Ernst Haas, who studied 137 disputes that were referred to the Organization between 1945 and 1984. Haas claims that the UN helped settle only 34, and in only 11 cases was the role of the UN 'substantial'. Another 40 conflicts were 'ameliorated' by the UN. Analysis by Brecher and Wilkenfeld (1991) seems to support Haas's conclusions. In an empirical analysis of 251 international crises between 1945 and 1985 they found that the UN's role was much less consequential than the roles played by the two superpowers, and the involvement of the UN was never the decisive factor in crisis abatement.

Such studies remind us that millions of people have been killed in violent conflicts whilst the Organization was confined to the touchline. We should also remember that many important peace initiatives have taken place with little or no UN involvement, especially when the great powers are involved in conflict. This led to the cynical comment by the Ambassador of the Ivory Coast, Arsene Usher, to the Security Council in March 1965. He stated that when there was a dispute between two small powers, the dispute eventually disappeared. If there was a dispute between a small power and a great power, the small power disappeared. If there was a dispute between two great powers, the Security Council disappeared.

Reforming the UN

It could be claimed that the UN has failed to fulfil the promise it showed at the start of the 1990s and this is, in many ways, more disappointing than its failures during the Cold War. Unlike the late 1940s, after 1989 it seemed that the Organization was well placed to play a significant role in world politics, since it was no longer paralyzed by the power struggle between the two nuclear behemoths. After 1945, it is now clear, the UN was fighting against the tide of international politics. In 1989 the tide seemed to be with the Organization. This suggests that the problems facing the UN are far deeper than just those associated with superpower rivalry between 1945 and 1989. There must be other factors that help to explain the continuing weakness of the Organization. Some of these are inherent in the nature of the international system and are beyond the ability of the UN to do anything about. However, there are also problems which the UN can address to make it a more efficient and credible actor. Three of these have received particular attention.

(a) Finance

The provision of adequate funding is a vital precondition for UN effectiveness, yet although governments are willing to give important tasks to the Organization they are reluctant to provide it with proper economic resources to carry these out. One recent example of this was the creation of 'safe havens' in Bosnia. These were established by the Security Council but UN members were then unwilling to provide the Secretary-General with the manpower to ensure the safety of the Bosnians in these areas. Lack of state support is also demonstrated by the fact that on 1 August 1996 more than 100 of the UN's member states owed the Organization over $3 billion, and more than half of this is owed by the US (United Nations, 1996).

Because the majority of members do not meet their legal obligation to pay their assessed contributions the UN is constantly on the verge of financial crisis. Simons (1995: 138) points out this problem and claims that 'The overall management task facing the United Nations is a nightmare. It is massively under-resourced in funds, personnel and general logistical support.' This, of course, may not be unwelcome to some powerful members who want to exert leverage to force through reforms of the organization. Radical ideas to reform UN funding include a tax on military budgets, a tax on air travel, a tax on postal services or a willingness to allow the UN to borrow money from international financial institutions (d'Orville and Najman, 1994).

(b) Quality of administration

Accusations abound of improper management practices, over-manning, fraud and waste within the Secretariat, the Specialized Agencies and in field operations. The impression remains of too many unread reports and repetitive and tedious debates that deteriorate into an 'orgy of rhetoric' (Kissinger, 1982: 1092). The perception of many is that the Secretariat combines 'patches of excellence with morasses of mediocrity' (Tran, 1995). Bad practice, and sometimes outright corruption, have also been a problem.

Some of the worst cases have been documented by Righter (1995). She points to the way that UNESCO was run under its former director, Amadou-Mahtar M'Bow, and the financial practices of UNHCR, whose director Pierre Hocké was forced to resign within three years of taking up his post. Roberts and Kingsbury (1994: 30–1) also mention western criticisms of Edouard Saouma, the Lebanese head of the FAO from 1976 to 1993, and Hiroshi Nakajima, who was appointed to take charge of the WHO in 1988 and whose re-election in 1993 was accompanied by claims of improper influence.

The large number of semi-autonomous specialized agencies creates significant problems of co-ordination and invites duplication, inter-agency rivalry and inefficiency. ECOSOC, which is supposed to help co-ordinate this system of autonomous specialized agencies, is not up to this task. The Secretary-General also finds it difficult to provide a sense of common purpose. He cannot appoint or dismiss the heads of these agencies or set their agendas. They also have independent budgets. 'Horizontal integration' can therefore be very difficult.

Findlay (1994: 28) notes that during the most recent phase of UN operations:

> Co-ordination of UN agencies in the field also remained problematic. . . In Cambodia, Bosnia and Herzegovina and Somalia, civil–military relations were at times 'strained'. Serious problems were also identified in the relationship between the UN's multiple humanitarian agencies and its political and peacekeeping structures.

Several informed commentators have called for a reform of this system. Notable past efforts include the study by Hill (1978: 91), which showed how the coherence of the UN system has been affected by the dispersal and fragmentation of authority. Comprehensive proposals for the reform of the Secretariat have also been put forward by Childers and Urquhart (1991). These include simplifying the chain of command, providing the Secretary-General with an Executive Office, and reform and reorganization of departments. The recent report *Our Global Neighbourhood* (Commission on Global Governance, 1995) has also identified several key reform ideas for the UN. It suggests *inter alia*: an enlarged Security Council with a possible phasing out of the veto; a revitalised General Assembly; a redirection of the work of the Trusteeship Council so that it would take over responsibility for the 'global commons'; the creation of a Forum of Civil Society to meet before each General Assembly session; the winding up of ECOSOC which, the report claims, has not worked, and the creation of an Economic Security Council; the closure of UNCTAD; and improvements in the procedure for appointing the Secretary-General. The Ford Foundation report (Independent Working Group on the Future of the United Nations, 1995) also calls for the creation of a Social Council to bring greater coherence to the UN's social tasks.

None of this will be easy given the way that the specialized agencies jealously guard their autonomous status. Here proposals for reform are not new. In the middle of 1997 Kofi Annan met fierce resistance over proposals to establish greater unity of purpose within a co-ordinated development group made up of UNDP, UNICEF, some economic departments in the Secretariat and the UN Fund for Population Activities. A proposal to close the Department of Humanitarian Affairs and to give its functions to the UNHCR also had to be shelved. Yet reform is essential; although the United Nations may not be the 'ineffectual, incompetent body unfair critics depict it to be, it clearly requires a serious overhaul to prepare it for the years ahead' (Kennedy and Russett, 1995: 71).

(c) Representation and legitimacy

Wallensteen (1997: 91–101) has noted that at present the west has 60 per cent of the permanent members of the Security

Council, whereas the third world possesses 20 per cent. The US is quick to criticise the 'tyranny of the majority' at the UN, yet seems blind to its own role in making the Security Council an instrument of a small minority. There are serious concerns in many third world states about the direction that the UN has taken since the end of the Cold War and a major worry has been the more interventionist Security Council.

From the perspective of some third world states the UN can be viewed as an agent of westernization, because of the way that the Security Council has been used in the 1990s to promote certain norms and to legitimize certain forms of intervention. They believe post-Cold War developments at the UN do not reveal a new era of multilateralism, but are a cover for western unilateralism.

The Security Council, as presently constituted, is not representative of international opinion. This, inevitably, has led to calls for changes to be made to the permanent members. Japan is an obvious candidate because of its economic strength and large contributions to the UN budget. In 1995 Japan was the second largest contributor to the regular budget after the US, contributing 13.95 per cent of the total. Since the Japanese parliament approved the International Cooperation Law in 1992 Japan has also been able to participate in UN peacekeeping forces, adding to its claim for a permanent seat. The first mission that included Japanese contingents was UNTAC, though – partly because of the controversial nature of this law in Japan, where opponents saw it as a manifestation of militarism – Japanese personnel kept a very low profile and remained rather inactive. As Japan searches for a new multilateral foreign policy more appropriate for the post-Cold War era, it is likely that its call for a permanent seat will become louder.

Germany is the third largest contributor (8.94 per cent in 1995) and also does not have a permanent seat on the Council. It could be that one way to involve Germany would be to have a European Union seat on the Security Council that would replace the representatives of the UK and France. However, this still does not include a permanent third world member, though Brazil (which had been proposed as a permanent member in 1945), Nigeria and India have all been mentioned as viable candidates. The UN has created an Open-ended Working Group on the Question of Equitable Representation on and Increases in the Membership of the Security Council and Other Matters Relevant to the Security Council, but its title hardly inspires confidence.

Another proposal is either to end or reform the veto system. The former is unlikely, since any decision to end the veto can be vetoed by any of the permanent members. Accordingly, interest has tended to focus on reform of voting procedures, which would leave the right of veto in place, but would require the votes of two or three permanent members to bloc a proposal.

The General Assembly can also be viewed as unrepresenta-tive. There are those who argue that the principle of 'one state one vote' is undemocratic because it does not take into account huge differences between states. Some commentators have suggested a weighted voting system for the Assembly that would take account of factors such as population and con-tributions to the UN budget. Another way of 'democratizing' the UN would be to create two General Assemblies, one representing states, the other peoples. Here the World Citizens Assembly has played an important catalytic role. Its Confer-ences on a More Democratic United Nations (CAMDUN) have provided important forums to push for the 'democratiza-tion' of the UN (Barnaby, 1991). Also of interest here are proposals to implement 'cosmopolitan democracy' at the global and regional level through greater use of the principle 'one person, one vote' (Archibugi, 1995). There are obvious problems with this proposal. How could the UN deal with undemocratic states that do not allow the people to choose their representatives? Even if a democratic 'second' Assembly could be established, Rosenau (1992: 69) warns that it might institutionalize and increase conflict rather than co-operation between a state-centric and a people-centric UN.

The Road Ahead?

The new Secretary-General, Kofi Annan, has already indicated that he is aware of the need for reform. In July 1997, six months after taking office, he announced a 'quiet revolution' at the UN that was composed of a number of initiatives: creating a development fund for poor states financed by the elimination of 1000 jobs and other cuts; mechanisms to ensure greater co-ordination between UN agencies; increasing the role of the UN High Commissioner for Refugees; and a stronger UN role in areas such as drugs, crime and terrorism.

The recent Ford Foundation report (Independent Working Group on the Future of the United Nations, 1995: 49) argues that a strengthened UN will be 'critically important in centring the world's attention' on what needs to be done to create a global society in which development, freedom and peace reinforce each other. Already the UN has played an important role in establishing global norms for human rights, environmental protection and the control of nuclear weapons.

Yet as we have repeated many times in this study, the UN remains essentially a state-based body and it is shaped by states far more than it, in turn, can shape international politics. This is unlikely to change in the foreseeable future. However, there may be positions between the UN as an instrument for the competitive pursuit of state interest and the UN as a torchbearer for global governance. Ray (1987: 378) notes that the Organization could 'facilitate the co-ordination of efforts of the world community to deal with problems that cannot be dealt with effectively by states going their separate ways'. Ramsbotham and Woodhouse (1996: 159) also see the UN as 'the framework for mutual accommodation of state interests' and 'as an agent for promotion of common interests and values'. Roberts and Kingsbury (1994: 73) reach a similar conclusion and argue that the 'UN is best seen not as a vehicle for completely restructuring or replacing the system of sovereign states but as ameliorating the problems spawned by that system's imperfections and as managing processes of rapid change in many distinct fields'.

It will probably, therefore, be business as usual at the UN, with perhaps a little more emphasis on the implications of globalization. This seems to be what most states expect from the Organization. If this assessment is correct it will continue to be an important meeting place. It will help to control and contain the destructive effects of the conflict inherent in a culturally diverse sovereign state system. It will help to manage crises when these conflicts become violent and destructive. It will help to co-ordinate responses to global problems and push forward with attempts to improve global governance. Finally, it will continue to be a forum where the poor of the world, often deprived of an effective voice, can try to pressure the rich into responding constructively to the 'silent emergency' of hunger and poverty. Whether the rich choose to listen is another matter. The signs are not encouraging: the needs of poor countries continue to be ignored and development remains the UN's 'neglected brief' (Adams, 1994).Compare, for example, the considerable western attention devoted to Boutros-Ghali's 'An Agenda for Peace' in 1992 with the disinterest that met his 'Agenda for Development' in 1994 and its recommendation that development should be recognised as the foremost task of our time. The reduction in the volume of assistance to the poor world also illustrates that the poor world finds it hard to interest the great powers in this issue.

Respect for state sovereignty remains the essential foundation of the UN structure. However, states do not always respect the UN in return and the Organization may not have the support of governments in carrying out the tasks they allot it. Article 2 of the Charter requires states to act in accordance with certain principles. Thus members agree to respect sovereign equality; to ensure to all states the rights and benefits resulting from membership; to settle disputes by peaceful means; to refrain from threat or use of force against the territorial integrity or political independence of another state in a manner inconsistent with the purposes of the Charter; to give the UN every assistance in any action it takes in accordance with the Charter and to refrain from giving assistance to any state against which the UN is taking preventive or enforcement action; and to ensure that states who are not members of the UN act in accordance with these principles so far as may be necessary to maintain international peace and security. Clearly states do not always respect these obligations.

Governments are very happy to use the UN as a 'depository of the world's lost causes' (Northedge and Donelan, 1971: 239) and then to blame the UN for failing to find the solution that has eluded them. They may also undermine UN actions by their own unilateral policies. For example, the permanent members of the Security Council have also been the states most to blame for providing a steady supply of weaponry to some of the world's worst trouble spots. The willingness of the larger powers to act unilaterally is revealed in the figures for Security Council vetoes. Between 1946 and 1996 these were used 238 times (116 by USSR/Russia, 70 by US, 31 by UK, 18 by France, and 3 by China).

Two other illustrations of this unsupportive unilateralism can be given. Firstly, in his account of his time as the US Ambassador at the UN, Moynihan (1975: 247) notes that 'the Department of State desired that the United Nations prove utterly ineffective in whatever measures it undertook. This task was given to me, and I carried it forward with no inconsiderable success.' Second, during a recent conflict between Iraq and the US over the UN's right to inspect sites in Iraq linked to weapons of mass destruction, Secretary of State Madeleine Albright responded to the deal agreed between Kofi Annan and Saddam Hussein in February 1998 by stating that 'it is possible that [Annan] will come up with something we don't like, in which case we will pursue our national interest' (*Guardian*, 23 February 1998).

Hammarskjøld once stated that the UN was created not to bring us into heaven but to save us from hell. As the peoples of Bosnia and Rwanda descended into their own infernos they could have been excused for lamenting that the UN had failed to do even this. Satisfactory explanations for this failure, however, must include an appreciation of the constraints imposed by the international context within which the organization has to operate. We should also emphasize that, despite these spectacular deficiencies, the UN is not bankrupt and can continue to make contributions to many diverse areas of world politics. The UN was born out of a tradition of thought about international relations that believes in the possibility of positive change in areas such as international peace and security, respect for human rights, and a reduction in the number of people suffering from hunger and poverty. It may not always be able to follow these goals effectively but they remain worthy aspirations, and as long as they are able to inspire or inform the work of the UN it will have a unique role to play in international politics.

BIBLIOGRAPHY

The works included in this bibliography should not be viewed as a definitive list of books about the UN

Abrams, Maurice B. (1979) Evidence to *House of Representatives Sub-Committee on Future Foreign Policy Research and Development*, 11 May–30 August, 1976. Washington: US General Printing Office.

Adams, Nassau (1994) 'The UN's Neglected Brief – "The Advancement of all Peoples"?', in Erskine Childers, ed., *Challenges to the United Nations*. London: Catholic Institute for International Relations.

Akashi, Yasushi (1995–6) 'The limits of UN diplomacy and the future of conflict mediation', *Survival*. 37, 4: 83–98.

Akehurst, Michael (1977) *A Modern Introduction to International Law*. 3rd edition. London: George Allen and Unwin.

Alger, Chadwick F. (1994) 'Citizens and the UN system in a changing world', in Yoshikazu Sakamoto, ed., *Global Transformation*. Tokyo: United Nations University Press.

Alston, Philip (1992) ' The Commission on Human Rights', in Philip Alston, ed., *The United Nations and Human Rights*. Oxford: Clarendon.

Amnesty International (1992) *Amnesty International Annual Report, 1992*. London: Amnesty International.

Archer, Clive (1983) *International Organizations*. London: George Allen and Unwin.

Archibugi, Daniele (1995) 'From the UN to Cosmopolitan Democracy', in Daniele Archibugi and David Held, eds, *Cosmopolitan Democracy*. Cambridge: Polity.

Armstrong, David, Lloyd, Lorna and Redmond, John (1996) *From Versailles to Maastricht: International Organizations in the Twentieth Century*. Basingstoke: Macmillan.

Augelli, Enrico and Murphy, Craig N. (1995) 'Lessons of Somalia for Future Multilateral Humanitarian Assistance Operations', *Global Governance*, 1: 339–65.

Bailey, Sydney D. (1969) *Voting in the Security Council*. Bloomington: Indiana University.

Bailey, Sydney D. (1975) *The Procedure of the UN Security Council*. Oxford: Clarendon.

Bailey, Sydney D. and Daws, Sam (1995) *The United Nations: A Concise Political Guide*. 3rd edition. Basingstoke: Macmillan.

Ball, George (1982) *The Past has Another Pattern*. New York: W. W. Norton.

Barnaby, Frank, ed. (1991) *Building a More Democratic United Nations: Proceedings of CAMDUN-1*. London: Frank Cass.

Beer, Francis A. (1981) *Peace Against War*. San Francisco: W. H. Freeman.

Bennett, Alvin Leroy (1995) *International Organizations*. 6th edition. New York: Prentice Hall.

Berridge, G. R. (1991) *Return to the UN: UN Diplomacy in Regional Conflict*. Basingstoke: Macmillan.

Bertrand, Maurice (1994) 'The Role of the United Nations in the Context of the Changing World Order', in Yoshikazu Sakamoto, ed., *Global Transformation*. Tokyo: United Nations University Press.

Best, Geoffrey (1983) *Humanity in Warfare*. London: Methuen.

Birgisson, Karl (1993) 'UN Good Offices Mission in Afghanistan and Pakistan', in W. J. Durch, ed., *The Evolution of Peacekeeping*. Basingstoke: Macmillan.

Boutros-Ghali, Boutros (1992) *An Agenda For Peace*. New York: United Nations.

Boutros-Ghali, Boutros (1992–3) 'Empowering the United Nations', *Foreign Affairs*. 71, 5: 89–102.

Boutros-Ghali, Boutros (1995a) *Supplement to 'An Agenda for Peace'*. UN Doc: S/1995/1.

Boutros-Ghali, Boutros (1995b) 'Democracy: A Newly Recognized Imperative', *Global Governance*, 1, 1: 3–11.

Boutros-Ghali, Boutros (1997). 'Empowering the United Nations', in Paul F. Diehl, ed., *The Politics of Global Governance*. (Boulder: Lynne Rienner).

Bowett, D. W. (1957) 'The Security Council', in B. A. Wortley, *The United Nations: The First Ten Years*. Manchester: Manchester University.

Boyd, Andrew (1962) *United Nations: Piety, Myth, and Truth*. Harmondsworth: Penguin.

Boyd, Andrew (1971) *Fifteen Men on a Powder Keg. A History of the United Nations Security Council*. London: Methuen.

Brecher, Michael and Wilkenfeld, Jonathan (1991) 'International Crises and Global Instability', in Charles W. Kegley, Jr., ed., *The Long Postwar Peace*. New York: Harper Collins.

Buchheit, L. C. (1978) *Secession: The Legitimacy of Self-Determination*. New Haven: Yale University.

Childers, Erskine and Urquhart, Brian (1991) 'Towards a More Effective United Nations', *Development Dialogue*, 1–2.

Clarke, Bruce (1995) 'Each State for Itself', *Financial Times*, 6 January.

Clarke, Walter and Herbst, Jeffrey eds (1997) *Learning From Somalia*. Boulder: Westview.

Claude Jr., Inis L. (1984) *Swords into Plowshares*. 4th edition. New York: Random House.

Claude Jr., Inis L. (1996) 'Prospective Roles for the Two UNs', *Global Governance*, 2(3): 289–98.

Commission on Global Governance (1995) *Our Common Neighbourhood*. Oxford: Oxford University.

Curle, Adam (1995) *Another Way*. John Carpenter: Oxford.

d'Orville, Hans and Najman, Dragoljub (1994) 'A New System to Finance the United Nations', *Security Dialogue*. 25: 35–44.

de Cuellar, Javier Perez (1991) *Anarchy or Order. Annual Reports 1982–1991*. New York: United Nations.

de Cuellar, Javier Perez (1995) 'Reflecting the Past and Contemplating the Future', *Global Governance*, 1, 2: 149–70.

Dallin, Alexander (1962) *The Soviet Union and the United Nations*. New York: Praeger.

Dedring, Juergen (1992) 'Silently: How UN Good Offices Work', in Elise Boulding, ed., *New Agendas for Peace Research*. Boulder: Lynne Rienner.

Donnelly, J. (1994) 'Human Rights and International Organizations', in Friedrich Kratochwil and Edward D. Mansfield, eds, *International Organizations: A Reader*. New York: Harper Collins.

Donovan, Robert J. (1977) *Conflict and Crisis: The Presidency of Harry S. Truman, 1945–1948*. New York: W. W. Norton.

Drysdale, John (1997) 'Foreign Military Intervention in Somalia', in Walter Clarke and Jeffrey Herbst, eds, *Learning from Somalia*. Boulder: Westview.

Eban, Abba (1983) *The New Diplomacy: International Affairs in the Modern Age*. New York: Random House.

Eban, Abba (1995) 'The UN idea revisited', *Foreign Affairs*, 74, 5: 39–55.

Falk, Richard (1996) 'Explaining the UN's Unhappy 50th Anniversary: Towards Reclaiming the Next Half-Century', in Dimitris Bourantanis and Maria Evriviades, eds, *A United Nations for the Twenty-First Century*. Hague: Kluwer Law International.

Fehrenbach, T. R. (1967) *This Kind of Peace*. London: Leslie Frewin.

Ferguson, J. A. (1986) 'The Third World', in R. J. Vincent, ed., *Foreign Policy and Human Rights*. Cambridge: Cambridge University.

Fetherston, A. B. (1994) *Towards a Theory of United Nations Peacekeeping*. Basingstoke: Macmillan.

Findlay, Trevor (1994) 'Multilateral Conflict Prevention, Management and Resolution', *SIPRI Yearbook, 1994*. Oxford: Oxford University.

Fisas, Vicenç (1995) *Blue Geopolitics*, translated by Andrew Langdon Davies. London: Pluto.

Fisk, Robert (1990) *Pity the Nation: Lebanon at War*. Oxford: Oxford University.

Fomerand, Jacques (1996) 'UN Conferences: Media Events or Genuine Diplomacy', *Global Governance*, 2, 3: 361–75.

Foot, Hugh (1964) *A Start in Freedom*. London: Hodder and Stoughton.

Ford, Alan (1957) 'The Secretariat', in B. A. Wortley, ed., *The United Nations: The First Ten Years*. Manchester: Manchester University.

Forsyth, David P. (1993) 'The UN Secretary-General and Human Rights: The Question of Leadership in a Changing Context', in Benjamin Rivlin and Leon Gordenker, eds, *The Challenging Role of the UN Secretary-General*. Westport: Praeger.

Forsyth, David P. (1995) 'The UN and human rights at fifty', *Global Governance*, 1: 297–318.

Fortna, Virginia Page (1993) 'United Nations Transition Assistance Group', in W. J. Durch, ed., *The Evolution of Peacekeeping*. Basingstoke: Macmillan.

Franck, Thomas M. (1995) 'The United Nations as Guarantor of International Peace and Security', in Christian Tomuschat, ed., *The United Nations at Age Fifty*. Hague: Kluwar Law International.

Galtung, Johan (1994) *Human Rights in Another Key*. Cambridge: Polity.

Goodrich, Leland M. (1976) 'Approaches to the Study of International Organization', in Avi Shlaim, ed., *International Organizations in World Politics Yearbook, 1975*. London: Croom Helm.

Goodwin, Geoffrey L. (1957) *Britain and the United Nations*. London: Oxford University.

Greer, Thomas G. (1958) *What Roosevelt Thought: The Social and Political Ideas of Franklin D. Roosevelt*. Ann Arbor: Michigan State University.

Gregg, Robert W. (1993) *About Face? The United States and the United Nations*. Boulder: Lynne Rienner.

Groom, A. J. R. (1988) 'The Advent of International Organization', in Paul Taylor and A. J. R. Groom, eds, *International Institutions at Work*. London: Pinter.

Gunter, Michael M. (1992) *The Kurds of Iraq*. New York: St. Martins Press.

Halberstam, David (1992) *The Best and the Brightest*. New York: Ballantine.

Hall, John A. (1996) *International Orders*. Cambridge, MA: Polity.

Halliday, Fred (1994) *Rethinking International Relations*. Basingstoke: Macmillan.

Hampson, Fen Osler (1996) *Nurturing Peace*. Washington D.C.: United States Institute of Peace.

Hannay, David (1996) 'Paying for the UN: A Suitable Case for Treatment', *World Today*, 52: 160–2.

Hannum, Hurst (1995) 'Human rights', in Oscar Schachter and C. C. Joyner, eds, *United Nations Legal Order, Vol.1*. Cambridge: Cambridge University Press.

Hart, Parker T. (1990) *Two Nato Allies at the Threshold of War*. Durham NC: Duke University.

Hazzard, Shirley (1973) *Defeat of an Ideal: The Self-Destruction of the United Nations*. London: Macmillan.

Heiberg, Marianne and Holst, J. J. (1986) 'Peacekeeping in Lebanon: comparing Unifil and the MNF', *Survival*, 33: 399–421.

Hill, Martin (1978) *The United Nations System: Coordinating its Economic and Social Work*. Cambridge: Cambridge University.

Hoffmann, Stanley (1968) *Gulliver's Troubles, Or the Setting of American Foreign Policy*. New York: McGraw-Hill.

Hoffmann, Stanley (1981) *Duties Beyond Borders*. Syracuse: Syracuse University.

Hoffmann, Stanley (1987) 'Is there an International Order?', in Stanley Hoffmann, *Janus and Minerva: Essays in the Theory and Practice of International Politics*. Boulder: Westview.

Hoopes, Townshend and Brinkley, Douglas (1997) *FDR and the Creation of the U.N.* New Haven: Yale University.

Hull, Cordell (1948) *The Memoirs of Cordell Hull, Vol. II*. London: Hodder and Stoughton.

Humphrey, John P. (1984) *Human Rights and the United Nations: A Great Adventure*. New York: Transnational.

Hurrell, Andrew (1995).'Explaining the resurgence of regionalism in world politics', *Review of International Studies*, 21: 331–58.

Ignatieff, Michael (1995) 'The Seductiveness of Moral Disgust', *Index on Censorship*, 5: 22–38.

Ikeda, Daisaku and Galtung, Johan (1995) *Choose Peace: A Dialogue Between Johan Galtung and Daisaku Ikeda*. London: Pluto.

Imber, Mark (1996) 'The Environment and the United Nations', in John Vogler and Mark F. Imber, eds, *The Environment and International Relations*. London: Routledge.

Independent Commission on Disarmament and Security Issues (1982) *Common Security: A Blueprint for Survival*. New York: Simon and Schuster.

Independent Working Group on the Future of the United Nations (1995) *The United Nations in Its Second Half-Century*. New York: Ford Foundation.

International Alert (1993) *Preventive Diplomacy: Recommendations of a round table on preventive diplomacy and the UN's agenda for peace*. London: International Alert.

James, Alan (1987) 'The enforcement provisions of the United Nations Charter', in UNITAR, *The Maintenance of International Peace and Security*. Dordrecht: Martinus Nijhoff.

James, Alan (1990) *Peacekeeping in International Politics*. Basingstoke: Macmillan.

Johnston, Harry and Dagne, Ted (1997) 'Congress and the Somalia Crisis', in Walter Clarke and Jeffrey Herbst, eds, *Learning from Somalia*. Boulder: Westview.

Johnstone, Ian (1994) *Aftermath of the Gulf War: An Assessment of UN Action*. Boulder: Lynne Rienner.

Kennedy, Paul and Russett, Bruce (1995).'Reforming the United Nations', *Foreign Affairs*, 74: 56–71.

Kissinger, Henry (1979) *The White House Years*. London: Weidenfeld and Nicolson.

Kissinger, Henry (1982) *Years of Upheaval*. London: Weidenfeld and Nicolson.

Knight, W. Andy (1995) 'Beyond the UN System? Critical Perspectives on Global Governance and Multilateral Evolution', *Global Governance*, 1: 229–53.

Kratochwil, Friedrich and Ruggie, John Gerard (1997) 'International Organizations: The state of the art', in Paul F. Diehl, ed., *The Politics of Global Governance*. Boulder: Lynne Rienner.

Kuper, Leo (1985) *The Prevention of Genocide*. New Haven: Yale University.

Kyle, Keith (1995) *The UN in the Congo*. Coleraine: INCORE.

Lerner, Natan (1980) *The U.N. Convention on the Elimination of all Forms of Racial Discrimination*. Alphen aan den Rijn: Sijthoff and Noordhoff.

Lewis, W. Arthur (1957) 'The Economic and Social Council', in B. A. Wortley, ed., *The United Nations: The First Ten Years*. Manchester: Manchester University.

Lie, Trigve (1954) *In the Cause of Peace*. New York: Macmillan.

Liu, F. T. (1990) *United Nations Peacekeeping: Management and Operations*. New York: International Peace Academy.

Luard, Evan (1979) *The United Nations*. Basingstoke: Macmillan.

Luard, Evan (1982) *A History of the United Nations. Volume 1: The Years of Western Domination 1945–1955*. Basingstoke: Macmillan.

Luard, Evan (1989) *A History of the United Nations. Volume 2: The Age of Decolonization, 1955–1965*. Basingstoke: Macmillan.

MacKenzie, Lewis (1994) *Peacekeeper: The Road to Sarajevo*. New York: Harper Collins.

Mackinlay, John ed. (1996) *A Guide to Peace Support Operations*. Providence, RI: Thomas J. Watson Jr. Institute for International Studies.

Bibliography

Makinda, Samuel M. (1993) *Seeking Peace From Chaos: Humanitarian Intervention in Somalia*. Boulder: Lynne Rienner.

Manikas, Peter M. and Kumar, Krishna (1997) 'Protecting human rights in Rwanda', in Krishna Kumar, ed., *Rebuilding Societies after Civil War*. Boulder: Lynne Rienner.

Matthews, Robert O. (1993) 'United Nations Reform in the 1990s: North–South Dimensions', in Gerald Dirks *et al.*, *The State of the United Nations, 1993: North–South Perspectives*. Providence, RI: Academic Council on the United Nations System.

Mazowiecki, Tadeusz (1995) 'Will to Disaster', *Index on Censorship*, 5: 67–72.

McCormick, John (1989) *The Global Environmental Movement*. London: Belhaven.

Melvern, Linda (1995) *The Ultimate Crime: Who Betrayed the UN and Why*. London: Allison and Busby.

Mingst, Karen A. and Karns, Margaret P. (1995) *The United Nations in the Post-Cold War Era*. Boulder: Westview.

Ministry of Defence (1995) *British Army Field Manual on Wider Peacekeeping*. London: Ministry of Defence.

Morgenthau, Hans J. (1967) *Politics Among Nations*. 4th edition. New York: Alfred A. Knopf.

Mower, A. Glenn (1985) *International Cooperation for Social Justice. Global and Regional Protection of Economic/Social Rights*. Westport: Greenwood Press.

Moynihan, Daniel P., with Suzanne Weaver (1975) *A Dangerous Place*. London: Secker and Warburg.

Nassif, Ramses (1988) *U Thant in New York 1961–1971*. London: C. Hurst.

Nicholas, H. G. (1959) *The United Nations as a Political Institution*. London: Oxford University.

Northedge, F. S. and Donelan, M. D. (1971) *International Disputes: The Political Aspects*. London: David Davis Memorial Institute of International Relations.

Northedge, F. S. and Grieve, M. J. (1974) *A Hundred Years of International Relations*. London: Duckworth.

O'Brien, Conor Cruise (1968) *United Nations: Sacred Drama*. London: Hutchinson.

Okoth-Ogenda, H. W. O. (1993) 'Human and Peoples' Rights: What Point is Africa Trying to Make?', in Ronald Cohen *et al.*, eds, *Human Rights and Governance in Africa*. Gainsville: University Press of Florida.

Parsons, Anthony (1995) *From Cold War to Hot Peace*. Harmondsworth: Penguin.

Prunier, Gérard (1995) *The Rwanda Crisis*. London: Hurst.

Puchala, Donald J. (1993) 'The Secretary-General and his Special Representatives', in Benjamin Rivlin and Leon Gordenker. eds, *The Challenging Role of the UN Secretary-General*. Westport: Praeger.

Quinn, John (1992) 'The General Assembly into the 1990s', in Philip Alston, ed., *The United Nations and Human Rights*. Oxford: Clarendon.

Ramcharan, B. (1987) *Keeping Faith with the United Nations*. Dordrecht: UNITAR/M. Nijhoff.

Ramsbotham, Oliver and Woodhouse, Tom (1996) *Humanitarian Intervention in Contemporary Conflict*. Cambridge: Polity.

Ratner, Steven (1995) 'The United Nations in Cambodia and the new Peacekeeping', in Daniel Warner, ed., *New Dimensions of Peacekeeping*. Dordrecht: Martinus Nijhoff.

Ray, James Lee (1987) *Global Politics*. 3rd edition. Boston: Houghton Mifflin.

Riddell-Dixon, Elizabeth (1993) 'North–South Relations and the United Nations', in Gerald Dirks *et al.*, *The State of the United Nations, 1993: North–South Perspectives*. Providence, RI: Academic Council on the United Nations System.

Riggs, Robert E. and Plano, Jack C. (1994) *The United Nations: International Organization and World Politics*. 2nd edition. Belmont: Wadsworth.

Righter, Rosemary (1995) *Utopia Lost: The United Nations and World Order*. New York: Twentieth Century Fund.

Rikhye, I. J. (1983) 'Peacekeeping and Peacemaking', in Henry Wiseman, ed., *Peacekeeping: Appraisals and Prospects*. New York: Pergamon.

Rikhye, I. J. (1984) *The Theory and Practice of Peacekeeping*. London: C. Hurst.

Roberts, Adam (1993) 'The UN and International Security', in Michael E. Brown, ed., *Ethnic Conflict and International Security*. Princeton: Princeton University.

Roberts, Adam and Kingsbury, Benedict (1994) *Presiding Over a Divided World: Changing UN Roles, 1945–1993*. Boulder: Lynne Rienner.

Robertson, Charles L. (1969) 'The creation of UNCTAD', in Robert W. Cox, ed., *International Organization: World Politics. Studies in Economic and Social Agencies*. London: Macmillan.

Rogers, Paul (1994) 'Renewing the Quest for Disarmament', in Erskine Childers, ed., *Challenges to the United Nations*. London: Catholic Institute for International Relations.

Rosenau, James N. (1992) *The United Nations in a Turbulent World*. Boulder: Lynne Rienner.

Rupesinghe, Kumar (1992) 'The Disappearing Boundaries Between Internal and External Conflicts', in Elise Boulding ed., *New Agendas for Peace Research*. Boulder: Lynne Rienner.

Russett, Bruce and Sutterlin, James S. (1991) 'The U.N. in a new world order', *Foreign Affairs*, 70, 5: 69–83.

Ryan, Stephen (1990). 'Ethnic Conflict and the United Nations', *Ethnic and Racial Studies*, 13, 1: 25–49.

Ryan, Stephen (1995) *Ethnic Conflict and International Politics*. Aldershot: Dartmouth.

Schacher, Oscar and Joyner, Christopher C., eds (1995) *The United Nations Legal Order*. 2 Volumes. Cambridge: Cambridge University.

Schell, Jonathan (1984) *The Abolition*. London: Picador.

Sherwood, Robert E. (1949) *The White House Papers of Harry L. Hopkins*. 2 Volumes. London: Eyre and Spottiswoode.

Simons, Geoff (1994) *The United Nations*. Basingstoke: Macmillan.

Simons, Geoff (1995) *UN Malaise. Power, Problems and Realpolitik*. Basingstoke: Macmillan.

Skjelsbaek, Kjell (1989) 'United Nations Peace-keeping and Withdrawals', *Bulletin of Peace Proposals*, 20, 3: 253–64.

Skjelsbaek, Kjell (1991) 'The UN Secretary-General and the mediation of international disputes', *Journal of Peace Research*, 28: 99–116.

Skjelsbaek, Kjell and Fermann, Gunnar (1996) 'The UN Secretary-General and the mediation of international disputes', in Jacob Bercovitch, ed., *Resolving International Conflicts*. Boulder: Lynne Rienner.

Skogmo, Bjorn (1989) *International Peace-keeping in Lebanon, 1978–1988*. Boulder: Lynne Rienner.

Stoessinger, John G. (1977) *The United Nations and the Superpowers: China, Russia and America*. 4th edition. New York: Random House.

Stremlau, John (1996) *Sharpening International Sanctions: Towards a Stronger Role for the United Nations*. New York: Carnegie.

Bibliography

Suganami, Hidemi (1989) *The Domestic Analogy and World Order Proposals*. Cambridge: Cambridge University.

Sutterlin, James S. (1995) *The United Nations and the Maintenance of International Security*. Westport: Praeger.

Taylor, Paul and Groom, A. J. R. (1992) *The United Nations and the Gulf War, 1990–91: Back to the Future?* London: Royal Institute of International Affairs.

Thompson, Kenneth W. (1978) *Interpreters and Critics of the Cold War*. Washington D.C.: University Press of America.

Thornberry, Cedric (1995) *Peacekeeping, Peacemaking and Human Rights. Occasional Paper 1.* Coleraine: INCORE.

Tinker, Hugh (1977) *Race, Conflict and the International Order: From Empire to United Nations*. London: Macmillan.

Tran, Mark (1995) 'Differing demands and varying goals bedevil secretariat', *Guardian*, May 20.

U Thant (1977) *View from the United Nations*. Newton Abbot: David and Charles.

United Nations (1990) *Towards peace in Cambodia*. UN Doc. DPI/1091.

United Nations (1992) *El Salvador Agreements: The Path to Peace*. UN Doc. DPI/1208.

United Nations (1993a) *United Nations Peace-keeping Operations*, Update 2. UN Doc. PS/DPI/14/Rev.4.

United Nations (1993b) *Convention on the Elimination of Discrimination Against Women*. UN Doc. DPI/993–98035.

United Nations (1994) *An Agenda for Development*. UN Doc. A/48/935.

United Nations (1995a) *Report of the Secretary-General Submitted Pursuant to Security Council Resolution 981*. UN Doc. S/1995/320.

United Nations (1995b) *Report of the Secretary-General Submitted Pursuant to Security Council Resolution 994*. UN Doc. S/1995/467.

United Nations (1996) *The UN Financial Crisis*. New York: United Nations Department of Public Information.

United Nations (1997) *Yearbook of the United Nations, 1994*. Dordrecht: Martinus Nijhoff.

United States Institute of Peace (1994) *The Professionalization of Peacekeeping: A Study Group Report*. Washington D.C.: United States Institute of Peace.

United States State Department, Bureau of International Organizations Affairs (1996) *Clinton Administration Policy on Reforming Multilateral Peace Operations*. Washington D.C.

Urquhart, Brian (1972) *Hammarskjold*. London: The Bodley Head.

Urquhart, Brian (1987) *A Life in Peace and War*. London: Weidenfeld and Nicolson.

Urquhart, Brian (1995) 'Between Peace-keeping and Force: To Fill the Fatal Gap. *The United Nations University: Work in Progress*, 14, 3: 3.

Usborne, David (1995) 'Unloved UN has unhappy birthday', *Independent*, 26 June.

van Boven, Theo C. (1992) 'The United Nations Secretariat', in Philip Alston, ed., *The United Nations and Human Rights*. Oxford: Clarendon.

Vincent, John (1986) *Human Rights and International Relations*. Cambridge: Cambridge University.

Vogler, John (1997) 'Environment and Natural Resources', in Brian White, Richard Little and Michael Smith, eds, *Issues in World Politics*. Basingstoke: Macmillan.

Waldheim, Kurt (1980) *The Challenge of Peace*. London: Weidenfeld and Nicolson.

Waldheim, Kurt (1985) *In the Eye of the Storm*. London: Weidenfeld and Nicolson.

Wallensteen, Peter (1997) 'Representing the world: A Security Council for the Twenty-First century', in Paul F. Diehl, ed., *The Politics of Global Governance*. Boulder: Lynne Rienner.

Weiss, Thomas G. (1995a) 'Overcoming the Somalia Syndrome – "Operation Rekindle Hope"?', *Global Governance*, 1, 2: 171–87.

Weiss, Thomas G. (1995b) 'The United Nations at Fifty: Recent Lessons', *Current History*, May: 223–8.

Weiss, Thomas G., Forsyth, David P. and Coate, Roger A. (1994) *The United Nations and Changing World Politics*. Boulder: Westview.

Whittaker, David J. (1995) *United Nations in Action*. London: University College London.

Woods, James L. (1997) 'US Government Decisionmaking Processes During Humanitarian Operations in Somalia', in Walter Clarke and Jeffrey Herbst, eds, *Learning from Somalia*. Boulder: Westview.

World Commission on the Environment and Development (1987) *Our Common Future*. Oxford: Oxford University.

Wortley, B. A. ed., *The United Nations: The First Ten Years*. Manchester: Manchester University.

Yergin, Daniel (1980) *Shattered Peace*. Harmondsworth: Penguin.

Zimmern, Alfred (1939) *The League of Nations and the Rule of Law 1918–1935*. 2nd edition. London: Macmillan.

INDEX

Index